Rancho Yucca Loma

Celebrity Guest Ranch and Hollywood Hideaway

Yucca Loma entrance, designed & built by Ernest Thompson Seton.

Dear Kathy,

by Fran Elgin

Enjoy!   *Fran Elgin*

Published by
Mohahve Historical Society
Victorville, California

D1225545

Rancho Yucca Loma:
Celebrity Guest Ranch and Hollywood Hideaway

by Fran Elgin, 2014

Cover design and photography work by Larry L. Reese
Layout by Beverly Huiner
Edited by Leslie Huiner and John Marnell

Printed in the United States of America

A Mohahve Historical Society Publication
Mohahve Historical Society, P.O. Box 21, Victorville, CA 92393
http:www.mohahve.org

Celebrating 50 years (1964-2014)!

The Mohahve Historical Society was established in 1964 when class members from a Victor Valley College History class who had researched and published a book of local history decided to form their own organization. The group has continued to hold regular meetings, go on field trips, publish local history books, gather historical materials, and promote knowledge of our rich Victor Valley history to the community.

Cover design: Front cover--Top photo is a painting of what artist Molly Kohlschreiber called the "Hobby House," also called "The Shop," with waist-high benches, and drawers full of arts and crafts equipment and materials, such as clay, wood and paper. Middle photo is a painting of Nini Barry's house by Ernest Thompson Seton. Bottom left is another view of the "Hobby House," a painting by Virginia Johnson. Bottom right is a broader view of the ranch by an unknown artist.

Back cover--The photo of "The Ark" and of a painting of Catherine Boynton were supplied by Evelyn O'Brien--origin unknown.

TABLE OF CONTENTS

FOREWORD

Fran Elgin, who moved to the high desert town of Apple Valley in 1963, taught at Yucca Loma School, and later earned her Library Science degree in preparation for a career as a Librarian. After she had worked at the Victor Valley College Library for a short time, in response to community and student inquiries, she started a collection of resources about the history of the Victor Valley and surrounding communities, including the Mojave Desert. Members of the Mohahve Historical Society contributed materials individuals had collected so that the photographs, books, and other historical documents would have a safe and secure home. When a new library building was constructed in 1997, a Local History Room was included in the plans. Fran has been an active member of the Mohahve Historical Society for the past 25 years, serving as officer and in a variety of other roles.

In the early 1970s, Fran's family wandered over to the nearby Yucca Loma Ranch to make a three-minute 8-milimeter film at the site where few of the abandoned buildings still stood. Her eldest son Jeff, with a painted on handlebar mustache, played the villain. Daughter Julie wore a long, prairie-style dress to portray the damsel in distress. They brought along a rocking horse for youngest son James to ride, while several neighbor boys joined in the action. Fran remembers the boys tripping in the desert sand as they ran to thwart the villain, who was tiptoeing up behind the heroine.

This history of the Yucca Loma Ranch is the result of Fran's fascination and love of the desert and her commitment to preserving the local history for future generations. Rancho Yucca Loma's story captures a sense of time and place when the high desert was remote but developing, wild yet serene, and a haven where even celebrities could come to relax and be themselves. It is also a testament to the courageous and adventurous spirit of the women who homesteaded and developed the Yucca Loma, and provides a snapshot of some of the colorful characters who were lucky to spend time here.

Leslie Huiner

ACKNOWLEDGEMENTS AND THANKS

When I started this project I knew I would need help, but not this much! When I was trying to place photographs in with text, I became so frustrated I almost threw up my hands. Fortunately, the talented Beverly Huiner, who has taught Business Education Technology for years at Victor Valley College, came to my rescue to help with the layout of the pages. Larry Reese, who had already helped with photos for two previous Mohahve Historical Society books, did more scanning and fixing for this Yucca Loma book. Leslie Huiner managed to find the time outside her busy schedule as Librarian at the college to scour the manuscript and catch my typos and other gaffs. I also want to thank members of the Mohahve Historical Society who have helped support and encourage me, especially Lorena Gragg, who was liaison with the printer, and John Marnell, another editor with an "eagle eye." Each one of these conscientious, caring people also offered suggestions to increase the accuracy and appeal of this book. And I am grateful to Dennis Casebier of the Mojave Desert Heritage and Cultural Association located in Goffs, CA, who informed me of the rich information that can be found in original homestead documents.

When Rancho Yucca Loma was in existence, and even after the buildings were deserted, local artists set up their easels to paint or draw some of the unique buildings there. Molly Kohlschreiber, long-time art teacher at the college, is now retired to northern California, but she graciously sent a photo of the painting of what she called the "Hobby House," which is on the front cover of this book. Joan Lopez gave me a note card with a drawing of the "Pueblo" by P. Nicholson (sp?). The painting of the "Pueblo" by Virginia Johnson is hanging in local "old-timer" Dick Garrison's living room at his Victorville home.

The naturalist, Ernest Thompson Seton, painted three paintings, including one of a fireplace, one of Nini Barry's house, and one of some other buildings. No doubt, there are more paintings out there somewhere. There are reports that the artist Trevor Bennett donated one or more of her Yucca Loma paintings to the Victor Valley Museum, but so far not one has been found.

Fran Elgin

INTRODUCTION TO YUCCA LOMA
Fran Elgin

In 1971 my family had been in Apple Valley just a few years, but we lived within walking distance of the abandoned Yucca Loma Ranch near Ottawa and Quapaw Roads. We took our children, ages 7, 4 and 3 there to walk around and wonder about the history that had been there. There was what looked like an old barn, and a small mortar and stone house. The *Daily Press* in 1968 had featured a series of articles written by Helen Berger, who recalled her years visiting the ranch and the many famous visitors she met over the years. As the first woman Bank of America manager in the Victor Valley and treasurer of the Red Cross Drive during World War II, Ms. Berger had become acquainted with Gwen Behr, the popular manager from the Yucca Loma who was known as *Mrs. Red Cross*. These articles piqued my interest, and I continued the curiosity for these past thirty plus years.

About eighteen years ago I met Evelyn O'Brien through our Mohahve Historical Society--a delightful, retired United Airlines employee who also had an interest in the ranch. Evelyn came to the college library to research everything on file there; she interviewed people who had been associated with the ranch; and she pored over old newspapers for news articles. Her intention was to write a history of the Yucca Loma, but unfortunately her health failed her and she passed away in 2000. Evelyn turned over her files to me, with the hope that I would carry out her dream. This is my intent.

Many of the photos in this book were from the Mohahve Historical Society's collection; some were obtained by Evelyn from people she interviewed; some were copied from Helen Berger's articles; some are from a history written by the daughter of one of the original homesteaders of the ranch, Ann Rivers Sudlow.

There are not many people alive who have memories of the ranch, but perhaps this book will stir enough interest to bring forth more stories and reminiscences.

WHAT WAS SO SPECIAL ABOUT RANCHO YUCCA LOMA?

Imagine Clark Gable or Loretta Young walking up the street in downtown Victorville, but no one asks for their autographs. Picture the Green Spot Cafe on Seventh Street, where famous writers and actors sometimes went to have a drink in the evening or to discuss the next play or movie script. In the 1920s, 1930s and 1940s, the residents of the Victor Valley were very much aware that one of the reasons some of the well-known visitors to the local ranches came to the desert was to get away from reporters and fans and have a relaxing weekend--or longer.

Compared with the glitz and glamour of the Palm Springs resorts, visitors to Victorville, Apple Valley, and Lucerne Valley were drawn to the more informal and laid-back atmosphere of the high desert, as well as the sparsely populated wide-open spaces. Each of the guest ranches in the Victor Valley had its own appeal. In the heyday of the Yucca Loma Ranch in Apple Valley, the Los Angeles newspapers published regular accounts of the comings and goings of the Hollywood set. According to *Los Angeles Times* columnist Hedda Hopper, one of the regular visitors, "Yucca Loma is the most unexpected place you've ever known…Gwen Behr won't take you in unless they know you…She wouldn't let *Life Magazine* take photos when they were there for the other ranches." Edwin Corle dedicated his 1941 book, *Desert Country*, to Gwen Behr and Rancho Yucca Loma. He described the ranch as "a paragon of a guest ranch--a design for living…" Mr. Corle had spent many vacations there, where he met his wife, Helen.

A dinner bell rang fifteen minutes before meals to call the guests to the Ranch House, where three meals a day were served at a sixteen-place refractory table. Ann Rivers, who grew up on the ranch, recalled that when she was fifteen or sixteen, the witty and creative conversation among the guests was a challenge for her to follow. The atmosphere was usually tolerant of controversial subjects, especially during the time of the McCarthy hearings, when many of the Hollywood people were supportive of the ones being accused, and others, such as Hedda Hopper, were ardent Anti-Communists. In her 1973 interview, Mildred Rivers DeMott mentioned that when tension mounted, they had a signal…"the silver saddle." She didn't elaborate, but that must have been a hint to change the subject. After the three courses at dinner with demitasse afterward, the guests sat around sharing the world news, joking, and gossiping. Games, such as charades, were welcome entertainment. Sometimes Gwen would play the piano. Bowling, swimming, horseback riding, and tennis were popular sports. Ann Rivers mentioned that Alice Marble, a top seeded tournament tennis player from Pasadena, taught her and her sister Bunny to play good tennis. A piano, drum, and a fiddle provided music for dancing at the American Legion Hall in Victorville on Saturday nights. Parties and visits to the other ranches were frequent. The rodeo in Victorville in the 1920s and early 1930s, then later at the Ihmsen Ranch in Apple Valley, drew thousands, including notables such as Rex Bell, Walt Disney, Jimmy Durante, Groucho Marx, Will Rogers, and hundreds more.

Between the 1920s and the late 1940s, Gwen Behr was the ultimate hostess, beloved by all, and highly respected in the community. Gwen was the daughter of one of the ranch's founders, Dr. Catherine Boynton. Although Catherine and her medical partner, Dr. Katharine Evans, started the ranch as a health sanatorium around 1918, their reputation for providing a healing place in a setting of clear air and wide open spaces grew to attract many rich and famous visitors over the years. Many took the train from back east, as the ranch became known for its stimulating but relaxing environment. The guest lists included artists and musicians, and visitors from Europe.

Many of the permanent citizens of the Victor Valley at the time the ranch was in existence never visited the ranch: for some it may have been a subject of curiosity, or even gossip, but it seems that most people accepted the Rancho Yucca Loma as a mini-community with its own contributions to the culture and image of the Victor Valley between the 1920s and early 1950s.

Helen Berger was the first woman Bank of America manager in the Victor Valley. When she first met Gwen Behr in the 1940s, Gwen was the local "Mrs. Red Cross." Helen became the treasurer, and they became good friends. Over the years, she became a regular visitor at the Yucca Loma. In 1968, a series of three articles by Helen and *Daily Press* writer Neal Sanderson highlighted some of the many interesting people who visited the ranch, and featured photos of the remaining buildings. In 1994, Helen spoke to Dr. Lyman's Local History Class at Victor Valley College about her wonderful memories and experiences at the Yucca Loma.

MAIN CHARACTERS

The purpose of the following list is to assist the reader in identifying these vital players in the story of Rancho Yucca Loma.

Dr. Catherine Boynton: Founder of Yucca Loma. Born Catherine White, she married Frank Boynton; then in 1917 she married **Lyman Thayer**, after which she was known as Catherine Thayer or Dr. Boynton. She did not have a medical degree but was trained by her father, Dr. Abraham White. Catherine was known as "The Healing Woman" or "The Praying Woman."

Harold Boynton: Catherine's stepson. **Roland (William or Billy) Boynton** was her son. Catherine Boynton's daughter, **Gwendolyn Behr**, manager of the ranch until her death, was married to **Herman Behr**, later divorced.

Dr. Katharine Evans: Never married, had medical training, shared Catherine's ideals of a place where people could come to heal. Dr. Evans' name appeared on most of the Yucca Loma related homestead records.

John Barry: Son of Nini Barry. Nini brought John to California when he was twelve years old because he had respiratory problems. John's sister Kitty Barry and Nini lived in Los Angeles but were regular visitors to the ranch, yet John lived there full time until he married. He started the *Victor Press.*

David Manners: A movie star who retired from Hollywood and built a house on the ranch. The house is still standing.

Ernest Thompson Seton: A famous naturalist, Seton and his daughter visited from New Mexico frequently. He designed the front entrance gate, and worked with John Barry to build an unusual house with Indian designs on the ranch.

Mildred Strong Rivers DeMott: Mildred's father, Frank Strong, helped Catherine Boynton locate the property where the ranch was built. Young Mildred and young Gwen helped the homesteading process by camping out on the site. Mildred's three children, Frank, Ann, and Bunny Rivers, grew up on the ranch. Ann Rivers married Peter Duval, who was killed in WWII. By the time she wrote her excellent manuscript of her memories of the ranch, her name was **Ann Rivers Sudlow.**

PROLOGUE TO THE YUCCA LOMA STORY 1903-1904

A series of strikes, known as the Colorado Labor Wars of 1903-1904, was one of the bloodiest times in Colorado history. In 1894 the Governor of Colorado, David Waite, had helped the miners in the first Cripple Creek strike win the right to belong to a union, an eight-hour day, and a $3.00 minimum wage.

By 1900 the ten towns in the Cripple Creek Mining District housed some 32,000 people. Most of them were miners and families drawn by the promise of steady work and good pay. The Western Federation of Workers were leaders in founding the Industrial Workers of the World in 1893. The unions provided for the health and welfare of its members, established libraries, and wielded considerable political influence. But their power ended with the 1903-04 Cripple Creek strike. The mine owners fought back by blacklisting the union members, and the newly-elected governor, Governor James Peabody, ordered the militia to support the owners.

A competitive group of owners had control of the mines, mills, smelters, and railroads. Many of them were anti-union. The militia arrested union leaders and denied them the freedom of assembly. A bomb exploded at the train depot, killing thirteen, and over two hundred union leaders were deported. Women became involved by fighting back. Their role in the reform movements had been huge. In 1902 women won an eight-hour day law for the women in Colorado, however, it was overturned by the Colorado Supreme Court. They played an important part in supporting the miners. Women had tipped the balance of the 1894 and 1904 elections that hinged upon the struggle between mine owners and miners in Cripple Creek.[1]

At the time of the 1900 U.S. Census, Catherine Boynton and her husband Frank Boynton were living in Cripple Creek, but by 1903 they were living in Colorado Springs. According to Catherine's 1924 biography, the 1903-1904 chaos in the mining community where she and her family were living had a profound effect on the young mother. She had been ministering to the needs of some of the women affected by the violence, including some of the prostitutes. She later recalled that around this time she had a vision of a peaceful place where she could provide spiritual and medical help to young women--a quiet place with wide open spaces. The violent conflict in the community was probably a contributing factor to the family's move from Colorado to California sometime before 1910. Catherine never forgot her dream, which resulted in the establishment of the Rancho Yucca Loma a few years later.[2] In Colorado, the family had lived in or near the town of Victor, the center for much of the violence. When she discovered the ideal site for her dream ranch in 1911, the location happened to be just a very few miles from the town of Victorville, a place that had been named Victor until the Post Office requested the name change at the turn of the century because of the confusion in mail delivery.[3]

Miners at the Vindicator Mine, Cripple Creek Mining District, Victor, Colorado, circa 1899.

NOTES

[1] *The Colorado Labor Wars, Cripple Creek 1903-1904: A Centennial Commemoration.* Edited by Tim Blevins, Chris Nicholl, and Calvin P. Otto. (Pikes Peak Library District, 2006).

[2] "Catherine Boynton," *Biographical Cyclopedia of American Women,* Vol. II, 1924, 44-48.

[3] Lyman, Edward Leo, *History of Victor Valley* (Victorville, CA: Mohahve Historical Society, 2101), 125-126.

THE MIRACLE ON MAGNOLIA AVENUE

It all came together on Magnolia Avenue in Los Angeles, where Catherine's neighbors played a large part in finding the ideal setting for Catherine's vision. On one side of the street were Nini Barry and her children, John and Kitty. Nearby were the successful real estate developer, Frank Strong, his wife Pearl, and daughter Mildred. Soon after the ranch was opened, John Barry became one of the first inhabitants of the ranch, where he lived from the time he was twelve until he married in 1948.

This photo shows a corner of a gable on Catherine Boynton's house at 963 Magnolia Avenue. On the bench are Nini and John Barry, with Catherine's son Roland in the middle. It seems that the Barrys lived in Catherine's house or were close neighbors. Across the street at 966 Magnolia Avenue lived Mertle Denny and her daughter Dorothy, who also soon became regular visitors to the ranch.

The author found Magnolia Ave. in Los Angeles, which is near the intersection of Olympic and Magnolia Avenue in what is now Koreatown. Most of the houses on the street have been replaced with apartment buildings.

This house on the corner of Magnolia Avenue and Olympic provides just a hint of how the neighborhood may have looked at one time.

THE BACKSTORY - OR HOW RANCHO YUCCA LOMA BEGAN

Rancho Yucca Loma began as a result of one woman's vision for a place for people to heal from emotional stress caused by health problems. Dr. Catherine Boynton had been looking for a place with wide open expanses, a peaceful setting, away from the stresses of city life. Catherine had the background of her early medical training from her physician father, Dr. Abraham White, when she was growing up. Then, while her deputized husband was involved in the Colorado Labor Wars during a turbulent time in the early twentieth century history, Catherine used her healing skills to help the families affected by the violence and lawlessness. After the family moved to California, Catherine found a place for her skills in a doctor's office in Los Angeles, and she became more and more determined to find the ideal location for her dream. Although she was in her thirties, and widowed (or divorced) with three children, Dr. Boynton persevered until, in 1911, she and her friends found the place near Victorville that was the beginning of what became the Rancho Yucca Loma.[1]

The Victor Valley in the early part of the twentieth century was a sleepy little community, except that it was a crossroad for travelers and trade. A few ranches and stagecoach stops had been established along the Mojave River. The railroad had been coming through Victorville and Oro Grande since the 1880s. By 1914, when the ranch began accepting visitors, train travel was cheap: round trip to New York was $118.50.[2]

The few dirt roads that existed were poorly maintained. Automobiles and buggies and horses were trying to meet the challenges of sharing roads. By 1913, there was only one automobile owner in town, so when the Seventh Annual Desert Classic automobile race from Los Angeles to Phoenix was routed through Victorville, Seventh Street was lined with spectators to watch the competitors, including Barney Oldfield, who won the race in his Stutz.[3]

A bridge for wagons and early automobiles at the Mojave Narrows in Victorville had been built in 1890, but failed due to poor construction. By 1909 the bridge was rebuilt, to last until the "rainbow bridge" (still standing) was completed in 1928. Before the present crossing was built in 1962, the road to Apple Valley came through the north side, then crossed over near where the Apple Valley Road now meets Highway 18.[4] When Dr. Boynton, her co-worker Dr. Katharine Evans, and others from Los Angeles came to the ranch, this road would have been their route after leaving the train station in Victorville.

Turner's Store on D Street in 1900.

Victorville Garage circa 1925.

DR. CATHERINE BOYNTON

Rancho Yucca Loma was founded on a dream of a self-made doctor/psychotherapist, Dr. Catherine Boynton. By the time an article in the *Biographical Cyclopedia of American Women*, Vol. II, 1924, was published, the ranch had proven to be a huge success. Most of the following chronicle of her early life is from that article.

In 1875 (or 1870) in El Dorado, Kansas, Dr. Abraham White and his wife had a daughter, Catherine. Catherine received her early lessons in service from her mother, but the training by her physician father enabled her to express it scientifically as well as emotionally. Dr. White realized that Catherine had been born with the gift of diagnosis, and he became her teacher. At the age of four when other girls were playing with dolls, Catherine was studying anatomy by the game of learning the bones of a human skeleton, and she never forgot what she learned about the structure of the human body. When she was ten years old Dr. White began taking his daughter, whom he called "Little Doctor," with him to make hospital visits.

Catherine married Frank Boynton, a mining engineer, and moved to Colorado. They had three children: Harold, a stepson, a daughter, Gwendolyn, and a son, William. After they moved to Cripple Creek in 1896 they found themselves in the middle of the bloody I.W.W. labor war. (*See Prologue 1903-1904.*) Her husband was made deputy sheriff, placing the family in midst of a community in chaos. Catherine nursed wounded miners and cared for their families. The women of the flourishing red light district turned to her for help. She was also a prominent member of the Women's Aid Society of the Congregational Church, where her husband was Sunday school superintendent.

One night Catherine rode into the mountains to nurse a sick baby in one of the miner's huts. While there she overheard a plot to trap her husband and prevent him from arresting a notorious gunman--leader of the moonshiners. Frank had told her that the gunman had been located, and warned her that if he failed to return by a certain hour to notify the authorities. Fearing for her husband's safety, she left the hut, jumped on her horse and rode to warn them. This done she started home, but found she had taken the wrong trail and was again climbing the mountain. Suddenly her horse stopped short. Recognizing an animal's instinct of danger, she peered down and saw they were standing on the brink of a rocky chasm with a sheer drop of many hundred feet. She looked out between pillars of rocks forming a natural gateway, and by the light of the moon saw limitless space unrolled before her eyes. That vast expanse, hushed and awe-inspiring, gave her a vision of what she had been seeking since childhood--a desert place for the body, rest for the mind and peace for the soul. Then and there she resolved anew never to rest until she had found such a place.[5]

The family moved to Long Beach, California, where they show up in the 1910 census.[6] (It is unclear whether Frank soon passed away or they divorced.) Catherine found herself in the position where she knew she had to make a living. While walking along the beach pondering her future, Catherine picked up a newspaper lying on the sand, in which an article on "Little Sermons on Health" written by a doctor caught her eye. She found the doctor's office and asked for a position in his practice. There she gained practical knowledge of how to treat patients, and she soon

CATHERINE WHITE BOYNTON THAYER

Catherine Boynton: Young Dreamer.

opened her own modest office to offer spiritual as well as physical healing. Too often her experience had shown her that after a surgeon had performed a successful operation, his patient needed mental as well as physical health. The doctors she worked with, although skeptical at first, noticed the improvement in many of their patients who were not recovering as soon as expected. They would refer them to "the praying woman." Catherine believed that healing by prayer is the scientific application of spiritual laws to mental and physical conditions. During the time she was in the office she met Dr. Katharine Evans, who had similar concerns. They worked well together, and would continue to be partners and friends the rest of their lives.[7]

Soon after she opened her office, Catherine's mind returned to the dream of a place in the desert where she could carry out her work. There are conflicting accounts of her first visit to the site where the ranch was eventually founded. In one story she was tipped off by one of her patients. But the story told by Ann Rivers Sudlow was that her grandmother, Pearl Strong, and Catherine were good friends and neighbors. Pearl's husband Frank had been in land development and real estate all his life. He was now based on Spring Street in downtown Los Angeles. Along with his partner, George Dickinson, they

were laying out a broad boulevard for prominent homes called Lafayette Park Place, and built a house on Magnolia close to where Catherine had bought a large two-story house in the same early California shingled style. Catherine went to Pearl's husband and explained her vision, and he agreed to help her find the actual land in the desert that matched her dream, including a knoll where guests could go to meditate. In 1911, Catherine, along with Frank and Pearl, took the train to Hesperia (or Victorville), then hired a buckboard and horse. They rode through the Mojave Narrows to the site.[8]

Dr. Catherine Boynton: The "Praying Woman".

Leaving the town they climbed slowly up the "grade" hewn out of the solid granite rocks. When they reached the top, she held her breath. Between massive pillars of rock, like another gateway, she found herself looking out over the wonderful expanse of the desert that lay before her. It was the place of her dreams. It was the vision of that night-ride in the Colorado mountains come true.[9]

Catherine knew immediately that this was what she had been seeking. She went back to Los Angeles, where she planned to file on the land the next day. Perhaps Katharine Evans was with her and they decided to file in her name instead of Catherine's. The earliest homestead records I could find were in Dr. Evans' name. By 1920, houses had been built and the ranch became a reality. Catherine married Dr. Lyman Thayer in 1917, and they bought more property surrounding the ranch as the interest grew and her family and friends were moving in.[10] They both set up practice in Victorville. Catherine's sons, Roland (also known as William or Billy) and Harold, visited the ranch frequently over the years.

After a lifetime of love and fulfillment, Catherine passed away in 1949 at the age of 79.[11] Dr. Lyman Thayer continued his association with the ranch and his practice in Victorville until the ranch closed. After he died in 1960 at the age of 80, his niece, Jean Thayer, formally dedicated the Thayer-Boynton Olympic size swimming pool at the Victor Valley High School in 1963. Funds had been raised in memory of Catherine Boynton Thayer.[12]

Dr. Lyman Thayer and Catherine Boynton married in 1917. Both cared for patients at the ranch, and Dr. Thayer had a practice in Victorville for many years.

Even as the ranch became known to Hollywood and New York people, Dr. Boynton and her friends and family always maintained the original purpose, "believing that the cry of every soul is for physical *Health*--mental *Peace*--and spiritual *Happiness*."[13] The houses and other buildings on the property were built around a mound called "the knoll." As Catherine wanted that to be a place for meditation and quiet, she never allowed anything to be built there during the time the ranch was active. Now there are beautiful homes on this gentle slope.

14

Left to right: Catherine Boynton and Gwen Behr. Looks like they're having a very serious conversation! Circa 1929.

Catherine Boynton and son William on "the knoll," circa 1930.

My dear Mr. Rathgan -

In according with your instructions I am sending the final Certificate, and reciept for my Homestead proof, with the request that patent papers be forwarded to me here.

I think I understood you to say that the papers would be ready in two weeks from the date of my visit to you bringing it to Tuesday May first - and that I might send in the final certificate if I were out of town at that date.

The business which summoned me from California still holds my entire attention, and I truly appreciate your courtesy and attention to this matter.

Respectfully -

Katharine Evans
17 Field Point Road
Greenwich -
Conn.

May 1st 1917.

A hand written note by Katherine Evans stating her absence from the homesteaded property—a requirement of the Homestead Act if not in residence 6 continuous months.

16

DR. KATHARINE EVANS

Homestead laws allowed American citizens over twenty-one to make a desert claim for land available through the government. Although homesteading had been available since 1862, it wasn't until the two decades after 1900 that most claims were made in the Victor Valley.[14] The *Victor Valley News-Herald* published numerous homestead entry notices each week, many for land in the area east of the Mojave River, now known as Apple Valley. Land was selling for $5 to $25 per acre. Well drilling was a thriving business. By 1917 the active Victor Valley Chamber of Commerce was already breaking into splinter groups that vied for government money and water rights.[15]

Homestead records show Dr. Katharine Evans as the person who obtained the first patent for the land where the ranch was built. Catherine Boynton had met Dr. Evans in the medical offices where she worked in Los Angeles. Dr. Evans became an unsung hero of the beginnings of the Yucca Loma. Homestead papers for Sections 29 and 30, T.5N, R.3W show that Dr. Katharine Evans paid $1.25 per acre for 160 acres, made entry in May, 1917, and received patent on May 9, 1922. She established residence on additional land in these sections in 1915, and built a house in October, 1915, as part of the homesteading requirements.

In 1915-1916 she put in about two acres of fruit trees--about half survived. In 1920 and in 1921 she cultivated about thirty acres of rye, but the first crops were destroyed by cattle, and some of the subsequent crops that were "growing, but rabbits eat it as fast as it comes up." A five-room frame house with board floors, garage, barn, and corral, a 295-foot deep well with engine and pump, as well as four one-room houses with toilets were added. One witness described the value of improvements as $7,500. Katharine, along with Dr. Boynton and her husband Dr. Thayer, homesteaded or purchased more land in the next few years, totaling 1,000 acres.[16]

According to Evelyn O'Brien's notes, the Virginia-born Dr. Evans was a Medical and Psychology graduate of Johns Hopkins University, which was the first medical school to require its students to have an undergraduate degree and also the first graduate-level medical school to admit women on an equal basis with men. (The school records do not show that she graduated from there, but perhaps her degree was from a different school). Dr. Evans never ceased to be intensely interested in the development of Victor Valley. She lived on the ranch during the 1920s, and hosted many visitors, including several visits from

Miss Florence Pennington, Secretary of the Children's Hospital in Los Angeles. Catherine and Nini Barry from Los Angeles stayed with Evans several times, as well as Pearl Strong and many other guests. In May, 1926, she was appointed to be on the board of the Mojave River Water District by the County Board of Supervisors. She maintained a home in Los Angeles, where she sometimes stayed. Dr. Evans died in June, 1944.[17]

Left to right: Reggie and Harold Boynton (Catherine's son),
Dr. Evans, Dr. Boynton, and Nini Barry.

Dr. Evans and others...Dr. Evans is second from left.

Dr. Evans, along for the ride in 1919. John Barry is sitting on the running board.

Gwen Behr in the 1940s.

Over the years, the driving force that kept visitors continuing to return to the ranch was Catherine's daughter Gwen Behr, who carried on the legacy until her death in 1954. Gwen and her best friend, Mildred Strong, played a big part in the original homesteading process, and continued to be involved for the next fifty years.

The 1900 U.S. Census lists Gwendolyn Boynton as seven years old and living with her mother Catherine Boynton, her father Frank Boynton, stepbrother Harold, and brother Roland (William or Billy), in Cripple Creek, Colorado.[18]   After Catherine brought the family to California, her daughter Gwen was sent to the Westlake School for Girls in Los Angeles for her education, where she met Mildred Strong. Catherine and Mildred's mother Pearl became good friends, and they were soon neighbors on Magnolia Avenue in Los Angeles, where Gwen and Mildred also became lifelong friends. Gwen graduated in 1911 and Mildred in 1912. Evelyn O'Brien was told that Gwen eloped with a handsome, popular football player, which was a "grand mistake" and was immediately annulled.   Mildred traveled east to Pine Manor, a finishing school. She found it stuffy and confining, and did not return for a second year.

By 1916, Gwen had gone east to New York to study piano at the Julliard School of the Arts.[19] The New York Social Register shows that in December, 1917, she married Herman Behr, a member of the celebrated New York "400," a list of the wealthiest New Yorkers.[20] As explained by Ann Rivers Sudlow, "Creative, energetic young married woman that she was, she started a ladies' designer dress boutique in New York." But soon she was found to be susceptible to pneumonia in the eastern climate, and the doctor recommended a dry, desert climate. Her mother Catherine and Catherine's new husband Dr. Thayer decided to build Gwen a house on the ranch, painted a rich sand color, where she could spend some lung-healing time. Gwen planned to stay a year. The Behrs in New York had made many friends in the theater, as well as the social realm. Many of them wanted to see Gwennie and "the West." So people would send a telegram ahead and arrive in Victorville by train. Telegrams were picked up often to bring the news.

Her husband, Herman, also visited frequently, and Gwen took the train to New York a few times. But soon Gwen found that the Yucca Loma was her home, and she became indispensable. Over the years, she and Herman visited back and forth, but were finally divorced in 1936.[21] In the 1920s, when he still visited, he was known to bring a suitcase full of gin with him, and walked to Miner's Hill (where the Hilltop House was later built), sometimes bringing one of the young ladies with him. Herman was not ungenerous. He financed the building of tennis courts and a swimming pool at the Yucca Loma. He had a guest house on the ranch built as a gift to Dorothy Denny and her mother in 1931. Dorothy and her mother were regular visitors to the ranch as they were good friends with their neighbor, Dr. Boynton, on Magnolia Ave. in Los Angeles. He also frequently visited Los Angeles, where he liked to stay at the Biltmore Hotel and took some of the young ladies to enjoy the night life.[22]

Gwen's friend, Helen Berger, said that Gwen was one of those wonderful people who could listen to your troubles and you would forget about them. When visitors had a problem, they would talk to her about it to get it off their shoulder, and then had a good time for the weekend. Gwen became involved in the community as well as running the ranch with her mother, who sometimes lived in Los Angeles. Accounts of the ranch by locals, as well as visitors from New York, Hollywood, and elsewhere had the highest respect for Gwen's mother, but they mostly agreed that Gwen's personality and genuine warmth, as well as her ability as a manager, were qualities that attracted visitors and encouraged lifelong friendships.[23] Many remember her colorful Southwest dresses and jewelry.

Gwen Behr with her brother Billy Boynton in front of the Victorville Garage, which was located near the train station.

In a 1998 interview, Allison Stockdale of Victorville talked about Gwen as a good friend. She said that Gwen would come to town in her big, open Packard convertible, with her big Alaskan Malamute dogs sitting there with her. Allison recalled that Gwen was always dressed flamboyantly; she would wear a bright scarf on her head and often wore velvet blouses and long skirts. Gwen would come to the railroad station to pick up guests, and she tried to talk Allison into starting a little tearoom by the railroad station where they could have tea and cookies. Allison liked the idea, but her husband didn't want her to do it.[24]

Johnny Barry wrote that the three Alaskan Malamutes had been given to Gwen by one of the men from George Air Force Base. But she let them just run in the desert and sleep wherever they chose, in the middle of roads or on footpaths. He claimed that the rancher Bob Hitchcock, who was a close friend, rode up to her door one morning and said, "Ms. Behr, sorry to wake you up so early but it's about them big dogs." Gwen noticed he and his friend were slouched in their saddles and were carrying rifles in boots hanging from their saddles. "Well, bad news--we came near shooting them." He pointed out that they were all matted from mud, as well as blood, because they had been killing his calves. She was shocked that her dogs had been guilty of being killers, and she sadly had them put to sleep.[25]

In 1953 Gwen had a stroke, and was sent to the hospital in Los Angeles. Helen remembers that Gwen called her several times and requested her to come down to see her. Usually when Helen got to the hospital Gwen would forget what she wanted. The last time was when she wanted Helen to do her Christmas shopping. Helen made up a list of everything Gwen wanted to get for everyone, but didn't do the shopping. She passed away in early January, 1954. When Helen heard the news she went up to the knoll and said her final goodbyes. Then she waited until it was time for everyone to arrive, and broke the news to David Manners, to Mildred DeMott and her husband, and her many friends. Mildred was also a good friend of Helen's.[26]

MILDRED STRONG RIVERS DEMOTT

Mildred Strong was an only child of Frank and Pearl Strong, born April 9, 1894 (Frank later remarried and had another child.)[27] Frank, one of the first developers of land in Southern California, had been looking for development prospects in the high desert when he learned of Catherine's interest in a place where young women could go to heal. He found 120 acres that had been turned back to the government and was available for homesteading. He and Pearl brought Catherine and Katharine Evans to the desert, where Catherine determined that this was a perfect place to fulfill her vision.[28]

In 1915, Gwen and Mildred were living a pleasant, social, and uneventful life. But everything changed when Catherine decided the two young friends would homestead 160 acres of the desert land! Although their names are not on the homestead records, in a 1970 interview, Mildred recalled how she and Gwen camped on the land in a tent for a year. They were required to eventually dig a well and plant some crop, which they decided would be barley. Once a week they would go into Victorville, rent a hotel room, take a bath, and wash their laundry at the Stewart Hotel. Since they had the room they must have also slept in a real bed.[29]

Mildred DeMott's daughters Ann and Bunny seeing Gwen Behr off to New York in 1933.

24

At first, they bought a mule, Nicodemus, and two water barrels to hang on his sides. They walked him two miles to a farmer to bring back water, but they remembered that he spilled a lot of water when he trotted wildly home. They then dug a water windlass well on the land, where they let a tub down and then cranked it to bring up perhaps four or five gallons of water. To spend a winter camping out in the desert may seem like a difficult challenge for two young women who had grown up in affluent households, but with their youthful energy and contagious enthusiasm, the plucky pair turned the dauntless task into an exciting adventure (at least in retrospect). Friends came out on weekends to share the adventure. Besides that, Mildred's father, Frank Strong, gave Mildred an impressive, open Buick Phaeton to use for exploring the desert or driving into Victorville.[30]

Mildred and her husband Henry Rivers had three children: Frank, Bunny, and Ann. Mildred built a small house on the ranch she painted white, called Casa Blanca. She later married Clayton DeMott, but she remained close to Gwen and the ranch, and eventually she and Clayton built a house down by the Mojave River called Meadowlark Farm. But when her children were young they had a very special childhood on the Yucca Loma Ranch. Mildred died February 4, 1973.[31]

Mildred Strong Rivers DeMott

25

PROGRAM
THIRD ANNUAL
NON-PROFESSIONAL RODEO

Anna Lou Rivers, Queen of the 1935 Rodeo, being congratulated for winning by
Rex Bell, moving picture star and one of our Judges.

AT SANTA FE PARK

VICTORVILLE - CALIFORNIA

October 17 and 18, 1936

Rex Bell, moving picture star and Anna Lou
Rivers, Queen of the 1935 Rodeo. The rodeo
was the second annual non-professional rodeo
and was held at Santa Fe Park in Victorville.

ANN RIVERS SUDLOW

Mildred's daughter, Ann Rivers, born in 1920, wrote about the wonderful memories of growing up on the ranch with her brother Frank and sister Bunny. They enjoyed exploring the freedom and uniqueness of the desert. They attended the Apple Valley School at Bear Valley and Deep Creek roads until they started going to the Victorville School once her brother Frank learned to drive. After graduating from college, Ann had many adventures, including being the second rodeo queen at the amateur rodeo held in Victorville. The first queen was Jean Campbell (later Jean DeBlasis) from the Campbell Ranch, and the third queen was Jeannie Godshall, who became a national champion. Ann was an accomplished horse rider, and she made sure her children learned to ride.[32]

WORLD WAR II

During World War II Ann married her bombardier husband, Peter Duval, but he was shot down in 1943 and was missing in action for the rest of the war before he was declared dead. So Ann moved back to the ranch with her baby son, Peter, in the spring of 1944. He was the only baby living there that summer. Her twenty-one year old sister-in-law, Susan Duval, came from Massachusetts to stay with them and got a job at the Victorville Army Air Field (later George Air Force Base). All the young women in town were very popular, as the USO was crying for ladies to come dance and entertain the men in uniform. Gas, butter, meat, sugar, and even catsup was rationed. Ann remembered a heightened sense of involvement, a moving energy. Dr. Thayer's clinic in Victorville was in tremendous demand with the many men and women from the base.

In her 2001 manuscript detailing some of her memories of the Rancho Yucca Loma, Ann Rivers provided a picture of what it was like during World War II. Gwen Behr was involved with the USO. She got the phone company to bus girls from San Bernardino for the dances. Usually there were about twenty girls to 200 men.[33] A November 12, 1942 *Los Angeles Times* article reported that when Gwen and a USO official planned overnight accommodations for seventy-seven girls from the Los Angeles Desert Battalion who came to Victorville for a weekend of entertaining the servicemen, the young women were guests at the Victorville Army Flying School after a dinner dance. "The soldiers remained to offer their services as bed-makers for the troop of girls. There were no complaints. Each bed was perfectly made!"[34]

Fourth from left, Gwen with men from George AFB in the 1940s.

Gwen Behr also headed the Red Cross, and worked closely with the sheriff, Zeke Eblen, to help people in trouble. That's how she met Helen Berger, who worked for Bank of America, and was the Red Cross treasurer.[35] In the early 1930s some aviators flew up from March Field in Riverside, waggled their wings over Yucca Loma, and then flew down to the alfalfa fields to land by the river, with Gwennie and Mildred driving down to gather them for lunch. One time Gwen invited the Air Force band to play at the ranch. After World War II came to Europe, and an airfield was built in Adelanto, Gwen was put in charge of the USO even before Pearl Harbor and the United States went to war. Everything changed, and Gwen's emphasis was no longer on guests. She rented every inch of space to the men at the base who desperately needed housing. Even "Mother Catherine and Lance moved from their home to their small house in Victorville, leaving their comfortable home for Colonel Paul Kirkpatrick." Pattie Squires, a colonel's daughter, came to work with Gwennie in managing the ranch, helping with grocery shopping, ration coupons, etc.

The ranch was functioning amazingly. But soon, Gwen's right hand man, Neil Hamilton, left for the Army, and Nat Joseph, the dramatic chef, was drafted. So, with only a mediocre cook, and no other employees, the ranch sheltered all these war-serving men. But the many wives helped by volunteering to serve, clear the tables, wash dishes, and clean up. They even scrubbed the pool, for no chemicals were ever used, and helped keep the grounds in order.[36]

One of the men from the base who spent a lot of time at the ranch, Paul Kirkpatrick, married another ranch visitor, Eleanor, in a sundown service in the poplar trees by the ranch house. After the war, Eleanor and Paul settled down in the Victor Valley and raised their two daughters. Paul was active in the community, and worked tirelessly to get a hospital in the area before St. Mary's was built in the 1950s. Paul passed away many years ago, but in 2013 Eleanor was living in Rancho Mirage close to her two daughters. The daughters were both surprised to find out, from a 1974 interview with Paul in the Victor Valley College Library, that their mother had been a plane spotter during the war.[37] Since this book was started, Eleanor passed away in October, 2013.[38]

Paul and Eleanor Kirkpatrick in the Ranch House on their wedding day June 17, 1942.

John Barry in the *Victor Press* newspaper office 1940.

JOHN BARRY

One of the first guests of the Yucca Loma Ranch was John Evarts Barry. John's father and John were both victims of the flu epidemic in 1918. His father died, and the family moved from Connecticut to California after their doctor had recommended a drier climate for John. His mother Nini Barry and John's sister Kitty Barry moved to Magnolia Avenue in Los Angeles about the time the ranch was being developed. Nini Barry became good friends with Catherine Boynton, who suggested that John would benefit from the climate at the ranch. According to Ann Rivers Sudlow, Mrs. Barry brought wealth and social standing with her. Many of Nini's contacts with the theatrical and art communities in the East became invaluable to the economy of Rancho Yucca Loma. The family spent summers in Nantucket Island for many years, even when they had homes on the ranch.[39]

Nini Barry, Billy Boynton and Catherine Boynton.

The twelve-year old John Barry took quickly to the ways of the west. He hiked across the desert to the one-room school house at Deep Creek and Bear Valley Road, a place that provided a fine view of the river. Later he rode a pony to school through the Ihmsen Ranch. Sometimes the cowboys on nearby ranches would let the boys perch on the corral rails and watch them tame the broncs and rope the cattle for branding. John enjoyed shooting rabbits with his .22 rifle on the way

31

to school. His little dog would trot ahead and try to menace the bulls on the range by barking and nipping at their heels. John claimed that sometimes the cowboys riding by would pretend that the children out for recess were runaway calves, and practiced roping them. Digging up arrowheads and metates in the dirt near the river with his friends was a favorite pastime.

As John grew older he complained to his mother about living in the same house as "those ladies." In 1922 when he was sixteen years old, Nini contacted her dear friend, the famous naturalist, artist, writer, and popular speaker, Ernest Thompson Seton, and asked that he design and build a guest house on the ranch for John. Ernest was happy to oblige, and John was happy to help with the construction. Indian symbols in the doorway depicted a buffalo head, a pine tree, and a standing man, representing the young John Barry. Seton's Indian name for Barry was

John Barry at his 1929 graduation from Stanford with Herman Behr, Gwen's husband.

Nibau, meaning "He stands up straight." Seton hired Mike, a Piute Indian from Victorville, to crack the colorful rocks for facing in the walls. When he asked Mike where he had learned to crack the rocks so accurately, Mike paused for a moment, and then replied "Folsom," and continued to swing the hammer.[40]

After high school, John attended Stanford University, where he majored in English and History. While at the ranch, John and his mother met the famed editor of the *Emporia* (Kansas) *Gazette*, William Allen White. Mr. White, a cousin of Dr. Boynton, made frequent visits to the ranch. John became his protégé, and it seemed that newspaper was in his blood. For a time he worked as a correspondent for the *Los Angeles Times* and the *San Bernardino Sun*. Through his mother, John also met many artists, scientists and business leaders.

John tried his luck at mining in Searchlight, Nevada, but decided the work was too hard for the return he got. Nini bought him a small cattle ranch in Yucca Valley, but that was not to his liking, so he went back to living on the ranch. In 1937, Nini and John bought the local paper, and he became the owner and publisher of the *Victor Press*, which enjoyed great success. In 1944 it had an average circulation of 3,000 a week. Publication grew from once a week to twice a week. In 1967 the newspaper changed its name to the *Daily Press*, which became a daily newspaper.[41] Nini died in August, 1955.[42]

Movie mogul Jesse Lasky and his family spent every other weekend in the winter at the ranch. Their teenage daughter Betty had never known a newspaperman before, and John was very kind to her. He took Betty with him as he toured around the Victor Valley gathering the local news--sometimes just how many eggs a farmer's chickens had laid. Then she would sit quietly in his little house while he typed the news. In the evenings, he would take her to the telescope mounted on the grounds, and explain the constellations. Betty Lasky said that John loved his newspaper. John did most of the work himself; he had one assistant--a female typesetter.

Nini Barry in 1940s.

Priscilla Lane surrounded by service men during WWII in 1943.

Actresses Priscilla and Lois Lane were among the many celebrities who visited the Yucca Loma. Betty Lasky said that quite a romance started between Priscilla and John, which was frequently mentioned in Hedda Hopper's gossip column. When the romance fizzled, some said that it was because John was concerned about becoming "Mr. Priscilla Lane." Others said it was because his mother did not approve of the gossip column notoriety or that she did not think a movie star wife was suitable. Another theory was that Priscilla had a drinking problem.[43]

In 1946, John married Elizabeth "Betsy" Thatcher Willis from San Mateo, becoming an instant stepfather to three. The Willis family were frequent visitors to the ranch. Betsy's son, Jack Barry, said that his father (Mr. Willis) always asked that should anything happen to him, his best friend (John) should marry his wife and help raise his children. After Willis passed away, the family continued to visit the ranch, and John and Betsy eventually married.

Betsy and the children moved to Apple Valley and quickly adapted to their new home. Jack Barry claims that John was the only father he ever knew. In 1946 Jack went to court and had his last name changed to Barry. The children joined the Scouts, and attended school in the Victor Valley.[44] Betsy became involved in the community by volunteering. She was a founder of the Apple Valley Country Club, wrote a column in the *Daily Press*, was an excellent tennis player and golfer, and had many friends. After John Barry passed away, Betsy stayed in Apple Valley until she moved to Huntington Beach in 2006. In July, 2013, Betsy celebrated her 101st birthday with her extended family.[45] She passed away on February 15, 2014.[46]

In the 1950s, John wrote two western mystery novels based on actual criminal cases. He retired from the newspaper in 1958, and continued to be active by teaching journalism at Victor Valley College. He passed away on December 31, 1995.[47]

Kitty Barry, Nini Barry, and John Barry in early 1930s.

Catherine Boynton, Ernest Seton and Gwen Behr 1929.

Nini Barry was on the board of the Woodcraft League in Los Angeles when she met Seton. Seton had founded the Woodcraft League of America in 1916 after splitting from the Boy Scouts of America, which he had co-founded in the United States. He had been chief scout of the Boy Scouts from 1910 to 1914, but he parted ways because he felt that the Boy Scouts had a military emphasis, while his organization incorporated Indian folklore, handicraft, and animal tales.[48] A 1928 letter from Seton to Nini Barry asks her opinion about moving the Woodcraft League headquarters from Connecticut to Los Angeles.[49]

Seton, who liked to be known by his Indian name, "Black Wolf," became convinced that the Indian ways of life were in many ways superior to those of the white man. After Nini Barry introduced him to the Rancho Yucca Loma in 1919, Seton became a frequent visitor to the ranch. His daughter Anya, also a writer, liked to visit with him. He was fascinated with the beauty of the High Desert, and gathered pieces of folklore from local residents for use in later magazine stories. Over his lifetime, he wrote over sixty books and short stories.[50]

In 1919 Ernest did a sketch for Catherine Boynton of a sanctuary she wanted to build on the ranch for herself. He supervised the construction of this tiny house she called "The Ark." It was her private place, and once she entered and closed the door, no one dared bother her until the door opened.

In addition to "The Ark" and the rock house, where John Barry lived, Seton designed the Kachina figures for the gateway to the ranch and supervised the construction of at least one other building. He also sketched a design for the fireplace in the main house, where he placed the motto: "Come Ye and Know the Peace of the Desert."[51]

"Catherine's spiritual philosophy, an all-embracing belief in the power of 'the other' spread gently into everyone, creating a rare atmosphere. Yucca Loma's peace and happiness pushed away the gloom of the Thirties Depression."- Ann Rivers Sudlow

---

Entrance gate with
Kachina designed and built
by Ernest Thompson Seton.

Seton with model of house designed for John Barry.

38

Seton house under construction.

"The weather at this desert retreat was mild to hot, sometimes 103 degrees in the summer, with a prevailing afternoon wind from 1 p.m. to 6 p.m., and a winter that had rain and occasionally snow, with sharp, cold nights and glorious black skies and millions of stars." - Ann Rivers Sudlow

NOTES

[1] "Catherine Boynton," *Biographical Cyclopedia of American Women*, Vol. II, 1924.

[2] *San Bernardino County Sun*, April 16, 1914.

[3] Edward Leo Lyman, *History of Victor Valley* (Victorville, CA: Mohahve Historical Society, 2010) 183.

[4] Lyman, 132, 193.

[5] Catherine Boynton biography.

[6] 1910 U.S. Census.

[7] Boynton biography.

[8] Ann Rivers Sudlow, *Rancho Yucca Loma* manuscript, July 2001, 1-2.

[9] Boynton biography.

[10] Marriage to Dr. Thayer in 1917 mentioned in Nini Barry's biography of Dr. Boynton (one page manuscript).

[11] Catherine Boynton obituary, *Victor Press*, July 1, 1949.

[12] Dr. Lyman Thayer obituary, *L.A. Times*, October, 1960.

[13] Boynton biography.

[14] Lyman, 149-150.

[15] *Victor Valley News Herald*, November 28, 1913.

[16] Katharine Evans homestead records obtained from National Archives.

[17] Katharine Evans obituary, *Victor Valley News Herald*, June, 1944.

[18] 1900 U. S. Census.

[19] Sudlow, 2-3.

[20] *New York Social Register*, May 1920, 50. "Herman Behr, Jr. married Gwendolyn Boynton, Dec. 1, 1917 at Greenwich, Connecticut."

[21] "Desertion Charged, Wife Wins Divorce," *The San Bernardino County Sun*, March 3, 1936.

[22] Dorothy Denny interview with Evelyn O'Brien in the late 1990s. Dorothy passed away January 8, 2007 at the age of 96. Part of her childhood was spent at the Yucca Loma; Obituary in the *Daily Press*, January 18, 2007.

[23] Helen Berger spoke to Local History class at Victor Valley College on March 17, 1994 on the subject of the Yucca Loma Ranch. VHS video on the VVC Library.

[24] Allison Stockdale, Transcript of 5/29/98 Interview #124 in VVC Library

[25] John Barry, *Early Days in Apple Valley, 9-11 (Unpublished manuscript)*.

[26] Berger talk to Local History class.

[27] Harriet Ryan, "A Big Donor Despite Dementia." *L.A. Times,* April 9, 2012. Feature article on Susan Strong Davis, Frank Davis' daughter, indicating she was a victim of financial mistreatment by a foundation. She was Strong's daughter by a later marriage.

[28] Sudlow, 2-3.

[29] Mildred DeMott, Transcript of 12/4/70 Interview #4 in VVC Library.

[30] Sudlow, 2. She was probably referring to the hand-operated device with a cylinder turned by a crank for hauling water in a bucket as illustrated. *Webster's Encyclopedic Unabridged Dictionary of the English Language* (New York: Gramercy Books, 1996.).

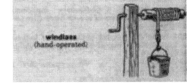

[31] DeMott obituary.

[32] Sudlow, 8.

[33] *United States Air Force Fact Sheet*, January 1991 [excerpt] (in Victor Valley College Library's Local History Room), "George Air Force Base was opened in June 1941 as the Air Corps Advanced Flying School. Later it was known as the Victorville Army Flying School, Victorville Army Air Field, and Victorville Air Force Base. It became George Air Force Base June 2, 1950, renamed in honor of Brigadier General Harold H. George."

[34] "Air Cadets Show Skill Making Beds," *Los Angeles Times*, November 12, 1942.

[35] Berger 1994 talk

[36] Sudlow, 10-11.

[37] Paul Kirkpatrick, Transcript of 4/9/74 Interview #59 in VVC Library, and email correspondence with his daughters in Rancho Mirage in 2013 and 2014.

[38] E-mail correspondence with Kirkpatrick's daughters, Joy and Jill.

[39] Sudlow, 4.

[40] Barry, *Rancho Yucca Loma*, 1-2. (Unpublished manuscript).

[41] Barry, *A Young John Barry Comes to Live at Rancho Yucca Loma,* (3 page unpublished manuscript.)

[42] "'Press' Co-Founder Nini Barry Passes," *Victor Press*, August 25, 1955.

[43] Betty Lasky Interview with Evelyn O'Brien in 1997.

[44] Barry, *A Young John Barry Comes to Live at Rancho Yucca Loma.*

[45] Lynnea Lombardo, "Wife of Daily Press founder turns 100." *Daily Press*, July 16, 2012.

[46] Rene Ray De La Cruz, "Daily Press Loses Founding Family Member." *Daily Press*, February 17, 2014.

[47] "John Barry, Founder of Victor Press, Dies at 89," *Daily Press*, December 31, 1995.

[48] Bil Gilbert, "Black Wolf." *Smithsonian*, July 1997, 110+

[49] Seton Jan. 6, 1928 letter to Nini Barry from Headquarters of The Woodcraft League of America; Also, a March 29, 1922 *San Bernardino County Sun* article reported that a Woodcraft lunch and program for Victorville high school students was held at the ranch.

[50] Patricia Morley, "Ernest Thompson Seton." *Dictionary of Literary Biography* 92, (Gale Research, 1990), 657-659.

[51] Similar to New Testament verse: Mark 6:30-32, "Come ye yourselves into a desert place, and rest awhile."

Ann Rivers Sudlow says, "On December 7, 1941, we were all at David Manner's [house], where we were enjoying the symphony and the radiant December sun, when Johnnie came pounding across the Ranch, sliding his horse to a stop in front of David's patio, and screaming, 'They're bombing Pearl Harbor! The Japs are attacking Pearl Harbor!' And the United States went to war."

Comfortable patio on western side of Manners' house.

DAVID MANNERS

Handsome, flamboyant, but down to earth, David Manners was a movie star who lived to be 98 years old. David claimed that the best years of his life were at the Rancho Yucca Loma, where he had his own little house built out of adobe in the early 1930s. He later described how wonderful it was to go to the ranch in its heyday. "Nobody interfered with anyone else--the houses were far apart." The ranch had a beautiful tennis court and swimming pool, in which the water was changed once a week and then used to water the trees. He said the "only road was over a hill and down a little path and up again, and suddenly you'd see that there was nothing for eighty miles in any direction but Joshua trees and cactus." He said the trees had a habit of dropping the seedlings, and there was an irritation in them. "If you walked too closely, they would throw the seedlings at you and you couldn't get them out. You had to go to a doctor to get them out."

He discovered Yucca Loma when a kind friend drove him up there one evening. When he was introduced to Catherine Boynton he asked her, "Could I build a little house on your desert?" She said "I'm in the habit of saying no. Come back next Sunday and I'll tell you." He had to wait a whole week because he didn't have a car. She told him to have it drawn up exactly as he wanted it to look and she would tell him if he could build or not build it. It was approved, and he hired the Burns brothers from New Mexico to build the adobe. He said they made the bricks from the desert dirt and put them on racks to dry for several months, where they sat there in rain and storms until they were waterproofed.[1] David was probably drawn to the ranch partly because of the spiritual nature of Catherine Boynton and the atmosphere that surrounded the area. He had studied religious and metaphysical writings most of his life. At one point when he was a young man, his niece remembered that he even considered becoming an Episcopal priest. Some of the books he wrote in later years were on these subjects.[2]

David was born Rauff de Ryther Daun Acklom in 1900 in Nova Scotia, but moved to New York in 1907, and when he was sixteen he acted in his first play at Trinity School. He remembered another Trinity alumnus, Humphrey Bogart, who was a year ahead of him. After serving as a cowboy guide out west, Acklom found his way to Hollywood. He met a director who persuaded him to come to the studio for a screen test. This began a seven-year career, in which he played opposite Katharine Hepburn, Loretta Young, Barbara Stanwyck and Claudette Colbert, along with several other stars. But after an "acrimonious spat" with Joan Crawford, he decided to leave the movie industry and spend his time in the desert home, where he settled in to write. He made a few more movies and television appearances in the 1940s before retiring for good. An early marriage to Suzanne Bushnell lasted only twelve months, but in

1944 he began a relationship with Bill Mercer, a writer, that lasted until Mercer's death of heart failure in 1978.[3] Bill and other friends were welcome at David's comfortable Apple Valley home over the years. Shirley Davisson and Dick Garrison, who grew up in the Victor Valley, remember visiting the ranch with their families, where David demonstrated the telescope on nights when there were few nearby lights to interfere with the view of the stars and planets. Robert Powell mentioned that David's description for the shadows on the mountains south and a little east of the ranch was "the elephants."[4]

David Manners at the Yucca Loma

1941-1942 photo of Pat Bergen's mother on a visit to the ranch just after she learned to drive, with David Manners. The German shepherd's name was Lindy.

Old-timers, such as Helen Berger and Ann Rivers Sudlow, had fond memories of visiting David's house on Sunday afternoons to listen to the New York Philharmonic on his grand, standing console radio.[5] After he moved to the ranch, he changed his name to David Manners, and wrote three novels. He also wrote a regular column, "Under the Old Yucca Tree," for his friend John Barry's newspaper, the *Victor Press*.[6] He purchased a 16-mm movie camera for $136.00 and began making his own productions, mainly chronicling life on the ranch. The first film, *Mojave Almanac*, starred Ann, Bunny and Frank Rivers. His last film, *Those Who Wait*, premiered at the El Rancho Theater in Victorville in 1945.[7] All the exquisite spots around the desert were in the movies, such as Deep Creek, and rides among the Joshua where the cattle roamed. Years later these films and the original projector were stolen from his home in Pacific Palisades. After the death of Gwen Behr in 1954, David moved to Pacific Palisades, where he lived until Mercer's death. His home on Rincon and Waco in Apple Valley was purchased by the noted singer John Charles Thomas. From there he moved to Santa Barbara, until his health went into a decline.[8] David passed away in December, 1998, at the age of 98.[9]

Young David Manners in his acting days.

Patricia Bergen spent time at the ranch from the time she was ten years old until she got married. After her mother's divorce in 1939 they came to the ranch to visit David Manners, who was Pat's uncle. Her mother got a job at Scripps College, and Pat spent her summers and vacations at the Yucca Loma, where Gwen was her "keeper and mentor." She claims that since she was an only child brought up with grownups, she was "probably obnoxious as all get out." Her mother never could pay her way, so she had specific chores, such as writing letters for Gwen, picking up groceries, assisting the maids, and helping at the USO. Yucca Loma didn't advertise their ranch as did the other guest ranches. Pat remembers that the rates to stay in the 1940s were $10.00 a day inclusive. Pat now lives in Tucson, Arizona.

Frank, Ann & Bunny Rivers at Deep Creek making David's movie.

Eleanor Kirkpatrick on Dude and Pat Mecklenberg on Pinto at David Manners' house, 1941.

EL RANCHO MUSIC HALL

Thursday Eve. Sept 21 '44

Overture.............."The Flying Dutchman"
Newsreel (Castle Films).............."D" Day

Yucca Loma Pictures

Presents

"THOSE WHO WAIT"

(A home-front album in Kodachrome, conceived, directed and photographed by David J. Manners.)

THE CAST

ANN RIVERS DUVAL
PATRICIA SQUIRES
LIEUT. CHARLES HODAPP
BETSY HODAPP
LIEUT. WILLIAM JOHNSON
PAT JOHNSON
LIEUT. WILLIAM CARTER
JUNE CARTER
HELENA MAY
PETER DUVAL, JR.
BETTY RIVERS
STEVEN RIVERS
GWEN BEHR
MARJORIE HYSLOP
PRISCILLA HOWARD
ELSIE MARTIN
LIEUT. MARY-JAYNE G. POINDEXTER
EDITH LEE
V. A. A. F. BAND
CADETS
G. I.'S AND OTHERS
"HANK"   "LINDY"

Rancho
Yucca Loma

SOUVENIR PROGRAM

"Those Who Wait"

A Word About the Picture

"THOSE WHO WAIT" is a sincere attempt to capture the mood of the ranch in war-time dress. But it is also intended as a tribute to the women who wait and keep the home front going.

The picture does not pretend to technical achievement. In this direction the limitations of a standard 16 m.m. camera, the absence of dissolves and fades are acknowledged. There is no "plot." The story is too well known, too obvious and too near us to record. Instead, we photographed, or tried to photograph between the lines.

The film stock for the picture was purchased by the ranch and the completed picture is the property of the ranch.

✤ ✤

Rancho Yucca Loma wishes to express its thanks for the hearty co-operation of the cast and also for the kind assistance of Lieut. Kenneth L. Harbert, public relations officer of Victorville Army Air Field, whose efforts in our behalf made certain shots in the picture possible.

✤ ✤

Performances after opening date by arrangement only.

Program for homemade movie, "Those Who Wait," taken at Deep Creek.

David hosting party, WWII.

NOTES

[1] http://members.aol.com/rickmckay/DavidMan.html, 7/12/2006.

[2] Interview via email with David's niece, Patricia Bergen, March, 2014.

[3] http://www.davidmanners.com/biography.html, 1/17/2013.

[4] Interviews with Shirley Davisson, Dick Garrison and Robert Powell 2013. They all grew up in the Victor Valley.

[5] Helen Berger spoke to Victor Valley College Local History class March 17, 1994 on the subject of Yucca Loma Ranch.

[6] Corle, Edwin. *Desert Country* (New York: Duell, Sloan & Pearce, 1941), 223.

[7] Ann Rivers Sudlow, *Rancho Yucca Loma*, unpublished manuscript, July 2001, 11.

[8] John Norris. *David Manners Biography*, accessed 2/9/2013.

[9] David Manners obituary, *Los Angeles Times*, December 26, 1998.

UNFORTUNATE MEN WITH FORTUNES

In the late 1800s, a tradition started in the eastern United States where some wealthy families who had young men who didn't fit into their lifestyle or for other reasons would ship them out west to live on dude ranches or other facilities and pay for their care. Because of her reputation as proprietor of the Yucca Loma Ranch, Gwen Behr, and that of her mother, Dr. Catherine Boynton, [known as a healer], several young men came under their care. There were some women too, but we don't have specific information about them.

Tefft Henry: In 1921, twenty-one year old Tefft Henry, whose family owned the Jewel Stove Company in Michigan, stood out, not only because he was 6'5" and 300 pounds. Although his mind had never developed beyond twelve years old, he was pleasant and friendly. Everyone loved Tefft. He lived in his own house on the ranch with a private nurse as supervisor and house mother. Most of the time he ate either in the kitchen with the other "children," or his house. On special occasions he ate in the dining room and was permitted to invite two guests. They were always the same people: Victor Valley High School Principal Keith Gunn, a fellow Scotsman, and George Tedburn of the Victorville Hardware. He developed a skill for photography, and loved to go to Big Bear to ski.[1] Locals remember his hearty laugh as he enjoyed the Saturday morning cartoons at the theater in Victorville, and treated fellow movie fans to candy and popcorn. His favorite cartoon was Woody Woodpecker, and Tefft would enjoy mimicking Woody's laugh during the shows.[2] Barbara Davisson remembered Tefft in logger boots, laced up almost knee high, and a beret.[3] Tefft had bagpipes and kilts from Scotland. He would frequently climb to the top of the mound and play his bagpipes. By 1956, after Catherine and Gwen had both passed away and the ranch sold, Tefft was sent to a facility in Vermont, close to the ski slopes. But there is no doubt that his best years were spent on the Rancho Yucca Loma.[4]

Bayard Gulick: Another man old-timers remember was Bayard Gulick, thought to be Gwen Behr's nephew; she made sure his meals and other needs were all provided for. For some time, he lived on the Yucca Loma Ranch, but old-timers Felix Diaz, Robert Powell, Shirley Davisson and Dick Garrison all remember when Bayard lived in an old shack near the railroad tracks in Victorville. One story was that he had suffered permanent mental damage when fraternity brothers at his college in Holland tied him to a windmill as an initiation stunt and forgot about him.[5] I heard a slightly different story from Barbara Sophy, who had heard the wealthy family who supported him was from

Los Angeles, and that he lived on the ranch for a while until his father could support him no more, so Gwen moved him to Victorville. Barbara also thought the windmill incident happened at USC.[6] By the time they brought him down from the windmill, the damage had been done. Mr. Gulick had been a brilliant student. While in Victorville he played the piano every opportunity he had, received about three foreign newspapers in the mail each day, and spent a lot of the time at the Victorville library, where Mrs. Ford was the librarian.[7] According to Felix Diaz, he never or rarely bathed, but he took his dogs on walks down to the river every day. He wore a coat and tie, even in the hottest weather. His meals were taken at the restaurants on Seventh Street, and once a month Gwen Behr would pay all his bills.[8] A 1918 article in the local paper mentioned that James Gulick of Coronado and his son Bayard Gulick had visited Mrs. Heinie Rivers in San Jacinto along with Dr. Evans, and Mrs. Garcelon.[9] A 1921 article reported that at a Father-Son banquet in Victorville, "Bayard Gulick, Tefft Henry and Noland Garrison furnished the instrumental music for the occasion..."[10]

There were probably others taken care of by the Yucca Loma staff, but these two are most remembered by the people in the community.

Tefft Henry was a huge man in many ways. He was always pleasant and full of life. Here he is posed with Princess Carol Marmon (1903-1966), heiress to an automobile fortune. She and her husband Nicholas Tchklotoua were frequent visitors to the ranch. Prince Tchklotoua was a Russian writer from the country of Georgia.

Tefft Henry with Bob Hitchcock.

Bayard Gulick at the ranch with his father (the remainder of the photo was damaged.)

NOTES

[1] Ann Rivers Sudlow, *Rancho Yucca Loma* transcript, July 2001, 4.

[2] Interviews with Shirley Davisson, Robert Powell, Dick Garrison and Felix Diaz, 2013.

[3] Interview with Barbara Davisson, 2013.

[4] Sudlow, 4.

[5] Felix Diaz, *Footprints from the Barrio* (Victorville, CA: Felix, Diaz, (2000), 201-204.

[6] Interview with Barbara Sophy, 2013.

[7] Robert Powell.

[8] Diaz, 204.

[9] *Victor Valley News-Herald,* October 11, 1918.

[10] The *San Bernardino County Sun,* February 17, 1921.

NOTE: The 1920 U.S. Federal Census lists a Ryard Gulick, 31, as a household member at the ranch. Tefft Henry is listed as a boarder at the ranch in both the 1930 and 1940 U.S. Federal Census.

New Year's Eve, small dining room, 1932.

New Year's Eve, circa 1937, 1938.

"There never was a 'bar.' But after dinner almost everyone stayed for fun and games. There was a piano--Gwennie would play, and 'Charades' was also a favorite."- Ann Rivers Sudlow

YUCCA LOMA RANCH STAFF MEMBERS

There was a parade of workers at the ranch over the years, temporary and permanent. One of the most memorable was Nat Joseph, the cook. Also mentioned was Neil Hamilton, unfortunately we only have first names for others, except for Pattie Squires.

Nat Joseph: After the first cook, Jimmy, left there was a brief intern cook. But then, Nat Joseph, a real chef with a background from New Orleans, was hired. When the word spread, many guests returned again and again, partly because of the terrific food served in the large dining room. Rosalind Russell was known to "plop down on the living room floor, banging up and down on her hips so that she could really indulge in Nat's delicious food." Hedda Hopper raved about the meals prepared by Nat, and when Gwen Behr died and the ranch was closing, she hired him to be her own personal cook. Bob Balzar, owner of a gourmet store in Los Angeles, who wrote a wine and food column for the *L.A. Times*, came to Yucca Loma to "enjoy Nat's magic."[1] John Barry remembered a birthday party for Beulah Bondi when she asked Nat to model her new red Paris-made tea gown. Nat, once a dancer at the Hollywood Bowl carrying African spears, appeared balancing the cake on a silver tray above his chef's hat. Beulah patted Nat's cheek and said, "Thanks dear, and my dress fits you better than it did me."[2] Dick Garrison, who grew up in Victorville and still lives there, remembered that Nat would drive to the train station to pick up guests in his bright red convertible.[3]

Nat Joseph, chef and entertainer.

Barbara Davisson said that Nat would chauffeur guests to and from the ranch to the depot almost daily. She remembered that he made regular visits to her family's Snell Dairy on Bear Valley Road to pick up dairy supplies for the ranch.[4]

Neil Hamilton: Neil was Gwen's right-hand man. He planned and supervised work for **Maria**, **Faustine** and **Tony** (no last names available). Tony lit the fireplace in the guest's houses. He also helped Faustine and Maria serve the dinner, passing the large, artistic plates that Nat arranged, to each guest. Ann Rivers recalled that Neil was a "charmer," who taught her and her sister Bunny to dance the Charleston.

Pattie Squires, a colonel's daughter, the only other staff member mentioned, was a pretty blond young lady who helped Gwen manage the ranch during the war, helping with the grocery shopping, the ration coupons, etc.

Neil Hamilton had left for the army, and Nat Joseph was drafted. They both returned to the Yucca Loma when the war was over.

But Ann Rivers Sudlow remembered that since Gwen was short on help, and she had rented every inch of space to the men at the Air Base who desperately needed housing, the many wives pitched in. They served meals, cleared the table, washed dishes, cleaned, scrubbed the pool after the water had been drained on the trees, and kept the extensive grounds in order. One of the Air Force men had been a clock jobber, so he willingly cleaned all the Ranch's clocks.[5] If any of the helpers were local residents, research has failed to uncover their stories.

Left to right:
Faustina, Nat, and Maria.

Nat the chauffeur.

NOTES

[1] Ann Rivers Sudlow, *Rancho Yucca Loma*, 8-9.
[2] John Barry, *Rancho Yucca Loma* Manuscript, 58-59.
[3] Dick Garrison, 2013 Interview.
[4] Shirley Davisson, 2013 Interview.
[5] Sudlow, 11.

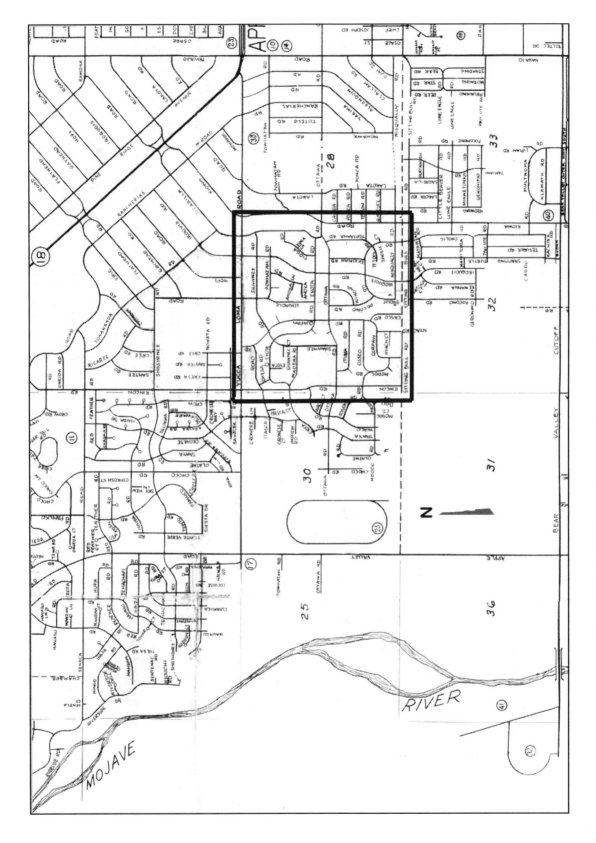

Map of Apple Valley with approximate area of ranch outlined, 1968.

BUILDING A GUEST RANCH ON A PIECE OF DESERT

By 1917, Katharine Evans, Catherine Boynton, and Lyman Thayer had homesteaded or purchased several acres of land in Sections 29 and 30, T.5N, R3.W in Apple Valley. They built a few houses on the tract and established residence, planted some trees and crops; and drilled a well in July, 1915.[1] The boundaries were roughly between what are now Kiowa and Rincon Roads and between Yucca Loma and Sitting Bull roads, although some of the buildings were in the area west of Rincon Road, including the David Manners' house at Rincon and Waco roads—sadly the only remaining structure from the ranch.[2]

Catherine and Dr. Lyman Thayer married in 1917, and they built the "Ranch House, a gray, wood-sided quarters for the communal kitchen, dining room, living room, two bedrooms and baths." In her memoir of the ranch, Ann Rivers Sudlow described the buildings that she remembered during the many years she lived there. Plans were drawn for a four-room house for Gwen Behr when she found that the climate on the Mojave was much better for her lungs than that of New York. In 1928 Mildred and Clayton DeMott built a two-room house they painted white and called La Casita Blanca. The walls were built with two-brick thickness and a space between them for air to circulate. In order to accommodate guests, a 100-foot by 50-foot reservoir was built above the ground to give movement and flow to the water as it was drained every week onto the many trees.

In 1919 Ernest Thompson Seton made the first of many visits to the ranch. Dr. Boynton requested a small house be built that she could use as a sanctuary, and for interviewing patients and/or guests. Seton designed and built a small, one-room house with an outhouse: the small structure was solemnly named "The Ark." Everyone knew that once Catherine went inside and closed the door to "The Ark" it was like hanging out the "Do Not Disturb" sign.[3] When John Barry asked Seton to design a house for him, he was happy to do so. The unique one-room house was built using the flat stones found on the desert surrounding the ranch.[4]

After Gwen's friends from back East started visiting for weeks at a time, Catherine chose an "American Plan" for Yucca Loma, requiring a rental agreement. "The ranch distinguished itself with three beautiful meals, all the recreational facilities, wood fires, and no phones [until WWII demanded a phone booth by the kitchen's back door.]" A bell tower with a train bell was rung fifteen minutes before the meals at the Ranch House.

More rooms were needed to accommodate the growing guest list. The Burns brothers from New Mexico appeared. First they erected "'The Big Adobe," that had a south bedroom and bath, a north bedroom and bath, and a recreation room in between. A large fireplace and ping-pong table were in the recreation room. The Burns brothers made adobe bricks 12" x 18" by 6", using the desert dirt and straw.[5] The next house they built, set on the west side on land off by itself, was for actor David Manners. Here the guests gathered on Sunday afternoons on his garden-patio, where they listened "to the New York Philharmonic on his grand, standing console radio."[6]

"The Pueblo" had four rooms on the south side of "The Knoll," with a wide space between where pine vigas made an informal portal. The two-room adobe on the west side near David's was called the "Little Adobe." Before the adobes a couple of one-room stucco houses were built--one for Tim Wanamaker and one for John's sister, Kitty Barry. A unique addition was "The Shop," with a workroom, waist-high benches, and drawers full of arts and crafts equipment and materials. A little laundry house held all of Gwen's brother's Blackwell law books in their lawyer's shelves, oak bookcases with glass fronts. A "string of garages were built on the south side of the pump house, and a small bath house for changing clothes by the steps leading up to the turquoise pool. The tennis court with the juniper windbreak lay to the east side of the pool. All flowed together in a friendly community way." Other buildings included a one-room stucco house built for the cook, Jimmy, and small quarters for additional maid help. Long-time resident Tefft Henry had his own house.[7]

Gwen's house, 1931.

"The Ark", Catherine's first home on the ranch.

Seton/Barry House.

The Ranch House, built circa 1920. View above 1965.

The Pueblo, circa 1940.

The Arts & Crafts shop, a.k.a. The Hobby House, a.k.a. The Shop, 1940.

The Big Adobe.

The Little Adobe.

NOTES

[1] Katharine Evans homestead records obtained from National Archives.

[2] Evelyn O'Brien's notes.

[3] Ann Rivers Sudlow, *Rancho Yucca Loma* manuscript, July 2001.

[4] John Barry, *Yucca Loma* manuscript, n.d.

[5] Sudlow, 6.

[6] Helen Berger spoke to Local History class at Victor Valley College on March 17, 1994 on the subject of the Yucca Loma Ranch. VHS video in the VVC Local History room.

[7] Sudlow, 6.

"THE KNOLL"

"The Knoll" was a low hill in the middle of the Yucca Loma Ranch property. In 1911, Dr. Boynton had found the land she had dreamed of, where she and her partner could provide a sanctuary for young women or others looking for a place to heal and find rest and peace in a place far away from civilization.

Catherine and her husband eventually built over twenty structures to accommodate the many visitors who came to this desert getaway over the next forty plus years. But from the beginning she determined that there would be no building on "The Knoll," as it was a place for solitude and meditation. All of the structures were built around it. Many of the people who lived there or visited mentioned this special place. Since the ranch closed, several beautiful homes have been built on what was called "The Knoll." It is hoped that the present inhabitants feel that same rest and peace that Catherine envisioned there.

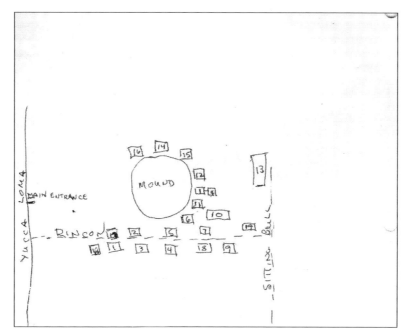

North   South

Rough sketch of ranch buildings. Date and
source are unknown. Key is not available.

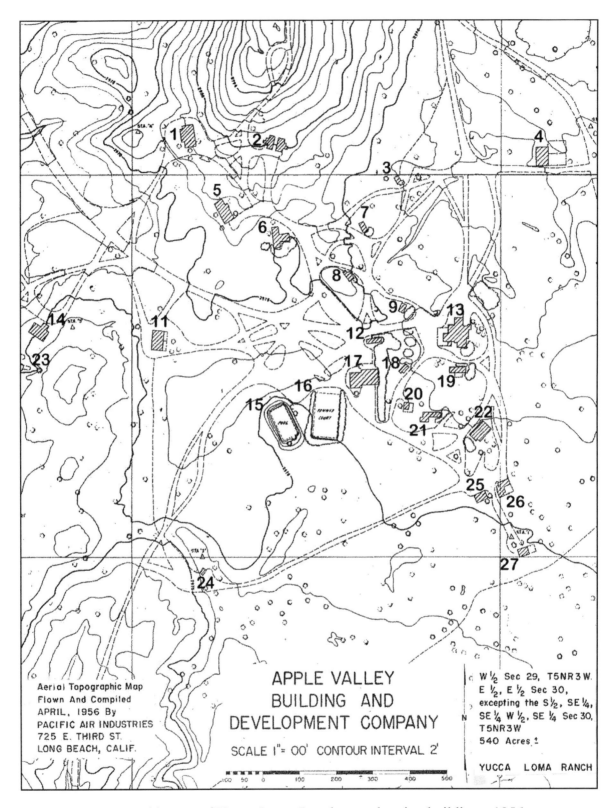

Topographic map of Yucca Loma Ranch area showing buildings, 1956.

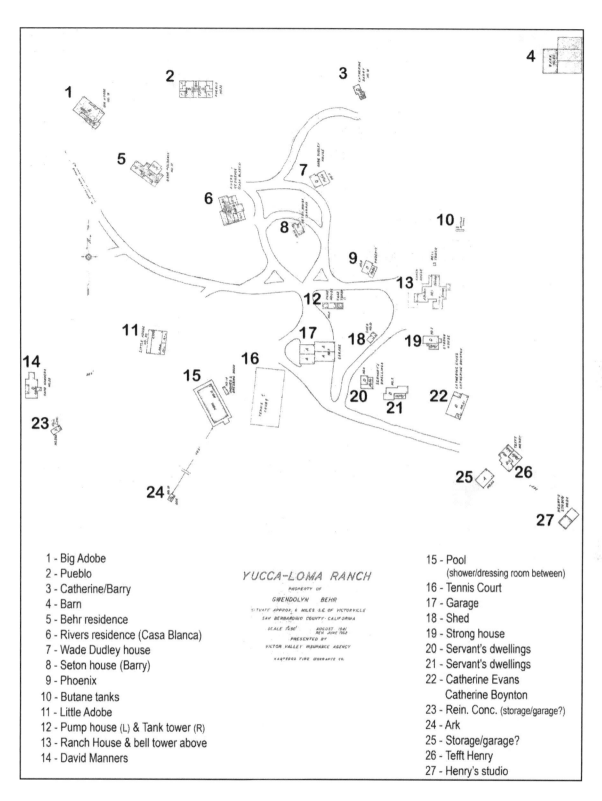

1 - Big Adobe
2 - Pueblo
3 - Catherine/Barry
4 - Barn
5 - Behr residence
6 - Rivers residence (Casa Blanca)
7 - Wade Dudley house
8 - Seton house (Barry)
9 - Phoenix
10 - Butane tanks
11 - Little Adobe
12 - Pump house (L) & Tank tower (R)
13 - Ranch House & bell tower above
14 - David Manners

15 - Pool
    (shower/dressing room between)
16 - Tennis Court
17 - Garage
18 - Shed
19 - Strong house
20 - Servant's dwellings
21 - Servant's dwellings
22 - Catherine Evans
    Catherine Boynton
23 - Rein. Conc. (storage/garage?)
24 - Ark
25 - Storage/garage?
26 - Tefft Henry
27 - Henry's studio

YUCCA-LOMA RANCH

PROPERTY OF

GWENDOLYN BEHR

SITUATE APPROX. 6 MILES S.E. OF VICTORVILLE
SAN BERNARDINO COUNTY · CALIFORNIA
SCALE 1"=50'   AUGUST 1941
                    REV. JUNE 1952
PRESENTED BY
VICTOR VALLEY INSURANCE AGENCY

HARTFORD FIRE INSURANCE CO.

Hand-drawn insurance map of Yucca Loma, 1941, revised 1952, 2014.

Carrie Jacobs-Bond and Dr. Catherine Boynton, circa 1911. A composer of some 175 pieces of popular sheet music from the 1890s through the early 1940s, Bond composed "I Love You Truly," a popular wedding song of that era.

VISITORS FROM STAGE, RADIO, SCREEN and TV

Movie star David Manners embraced the peace of Rancho Yucca Loma to the extent he left Hollywood and became a permanent resident in the 1930s. Hundreds of actors, movie writers, directors, producers, and others connected with the entertainment industry visited the ranch, especially during the 1920s, 1930s, and 1940s. The word spread that this was a rugged, quiet place of solace surrounded with Joshua trees and spacious views within driving distance from Los Angeles--or a few days travel on the train from New York, where Broadway creative people came to see for themselves what all the fuss was about. The contrast with that other desert getaway, Palm Springs, where glitter and night clubs were the attraction, was striking. Due to the legendary hospitality of Dr. Boynton and Gwen Behr and the high desert attractions, many guests made multiple visits to the Rancho Yucca Loma. Several people who shared their memories expressed regret that the large wood, leather-covered guest book with all the signatures and fond messages from the hundreds of guests never turned up. Some thought that David Manners had it, but he later denied it. Here are a few guests who made impressions on those who wrote about or told of their memories.

George Abbott (1887-1995) - In her memories of life on the ranch, Ann Sudlow says that she remembered George Abbott as a regular visitor, but it wasn't until a few years later that she found out he was well-known in Broadway at the time of his visits. He started acting in plays in 1913, and soon began to write. He moved to Hollywood, where he was a writer and director. He remained active past his 100th birthday by golfing and dancing. In his obituary, his wife stated that he was dictating revisions to *Pajama Game* and working on a revival of *Damn Yankees* just a week and a half before his death.[1]

Maude Adams (1872-1953) - Maude Adams was first well-known for playing the role of Peter Pan on Broadway. She went on to perform in other stage productions, with James Barrie's *A Kiss for Cinderella*, her final off-Broadway play in 1916. She appeared in several Shakespeare plays, and taught acting in Missouri. She died in 1953 in New York, but Helen Berger remembers her visits to the ranch in her later years. In one of Hedda Hopper's columns she mentioned that Maude fell in love with the desert. She got up "before every sunrise and watched every sunset until the last visage of color left the sky." Hopper quoted that Maude said, "I never felt so close to God before. There you could see the hand of God at work."[2]

67

Eddie "Rochester" Anderson (1905-1977) - Anderson had been an actor and vaudeville performer before he was hired as a train porter in 1937 for the *Jack Benny Radio Show*. The role of Rochester was to be a one-shot appearance, but the audience response was so favorable the script writers had Benny hire him away from the railroad to become his valet and butler. His distinctive raspy voice was a result of shouting all day to sell newspapers in San Francisco when he was twelve years old. The character became almost as popular as Jack Benny himself. The radio show ran from 1937-49, and the television show from 1953-65. He made several movies, not all of them with Benny. Although the role of servant and master was based on a racial stereotype, there were few complaints from either black or white audiences because Rochester always got the best of Benny on the show. But by 1965 the portrayal of the stereotype, no matter how benign the intention, was no longer accepted as the norm. When Rochester visited the high desert to make the movie, *Buck Benny Rides Again*, he stayed at the Murray Ranch or at the Yucca Loma with his friend Nat Joseph.[3]

Dorothy Arzner (1897-1979) - Dorothy Arzner was a film director. From the late 1920s until the early 1940s she was the only woman director working in feature films. After going to medical school at USC, she left school to work in the ambulance corps during World War I. Then she got a job as a stenographer at Paramount Pictures, where she moved on to script writer, and was soon promoted to film editor, where she excelled as writer and editor for over fifty more films. She was given a directorial position after she threatened to move to rival Columbia Studios. Many of her films featured free-spirited, independent women. By 1943 she was directing television commercials and Army training films. She later taught screenwriting and directing at the UCLA film school until her death in 1979. She was known to always dress like a man with a man's haircut, despite the studio's encouragement to wear dresses and have a more feminine hair style, and they made an effort to publicize that she had boyfriends. Dorothy was a long-time friend of Gwen and Mildred from when they had been classmates at the Westlake School for Girls. She made frequent visits to the ranch with her friend Marion Morgan, choreographer of the famous Marion Morgan Dancers. They lived together in the Hollywood Hills for over forty years until Marion's death in 1971.[4]

Sy Bartlett (1900-1978) - Sy Bartlett was a screenwriter/producer of Hollywood films, where he first wrote twenty-eight screenplays from 1933 to 1969. In the 1950s he began producing films. When he was assigned to the Army Pictorial Service during World War II he met Beirne Lay, and in 1946 the partners began writing a book about their experiences and observations from when they were both assigned to the Eighth Air Force in England. *Twelve O'Clock High*, the novel, was completed in 1948, and then they wrote the movie script, completing it in 1949. The movie, *Twelve O'Clock High*, released in early 1950, was an instant hit, earning several Academy Awards. In 1998, the film was selected for preservation in the National Film Registry as being "culturally, historically, or aesthetically significant." According to Ann Sudlow, much of the writing was done at the ranch. She claimed that when Sy would get too verbose, the fly boys would mutter, "Bail out, Sy, bail out." Ann mentioned that Sy tried to teach her and her brother Frank how to play polo on their easygoing trail horses.[5]

Jack Benny (1894-1974) - Benny took violin lessons as a child, and showed so much talent that for a time he wanted to be a concert artist. When he was seventeen he was expelled from school because he took afternoons off to play in matinees at the local theater's orchestra. From 1932 to 1955 his radio show was popular, and by 1955 he moved to television, which became a weekly feature in 1960. He was the first comedian to share laughs with his fellow cast members. Eddie "Rochester" Anderson, Dennis Day, and Don Wilson became almost as famous as he was. Benny was in several movies. The 1940 movie *Buck Benny Rides Again,* at least partially filmed in the Victor Valley, featured Andy Divine, Phil Harris, and most of the characters associated with the radio show. According to the *Victor Press*, "the company of over 100, along with dozens of trucks and livestock, was expected to stay about a week." Benny and most of the producers, directors, cameramen and sound technicians stayed at the C Bar G ranch in Victorville. Others stayed at the Green Spot, the Smith or the Stewart Hotel in Victorville.[6]

Carrie Bond (1862-1946) - Carrie Jacobs-Bond composed some 175 pieces of popular sheet music from the 1890s through the early 1940s. She had a son and an early divorce. After her second husband died in an accident, she was forced to earn a living with her music. Because her attempts to have her sheet music published were repeatedly turned down by the male-dominated music industry of the day, she established her own publishing company in 1896, resulting in her ownership of every song she had written. "I Love You Truly," which became a favorite as a wedding song, first appeared in her 1901 collection, and sold over one million copies. But the song with the highest number of sales was "A Perfect Day." In later years she recalled that she wrote the music for the song during a moonlight drive across the Mojave Desert. Helen Berger remembered that Carrie told her that once when she was in Paris she was told by someone that "A Perfect Day" was so popular in France he thought it was our national anthem.[7]

Beulah Bondi (1889-1991) - The character actress, Beulah Bondi, was born in Chicago in 1889, and was an established, successful stage actress before she made her first movie in 1931 at the age of forty-three. She was typecast as a mother or grandmother in most of the movies, most notably as James Stewart's mother "Ma Bailey" in the movie *It's a Wonderful Life* in 1946. Besides several mentions in Hedda Hopper's columns, Beulah was remembered by Ann Sudlow, who said that "Beulah Bondi and Helen Freeman…arrived so often we thought of them as part of the ranch 'family.' Beulah had a marvelous sense of humor." Helen Berger recalled that Beulah and Nini Barry had a long-standing game of Chinese Checkers every New Year's Eve. She also "played a three-deck game of Canasta that nobody could figure out unless Beulah was there to tell them the rules." Beulah died at the age of 92 after she broke her ribs when she tripped over her cat.[8]

Marge and Gower Champion - Both Marge (1919-   ) and Gower (1921-1980) were accomplished dancers before they met. They teamed up and married in 1947, but their success as "Marge and Gower Champion" won them awards, and soon they were appearing on shows, such as a TV series with Sid Caesar and Imogene Coca. They were in several musicals and special appearances before their divorce in 1973. When they visited the ranch it was in the late 1940s or early 1950s.[9]

Clark Gable (1901-1960) - One of the favorite celebrities to visit the Victor Valley was Clark Gable, the handsome movie star who was in over sixty movies in his relatively short lifetime, including *Gone with the Wind*, *Mutiny on the Bounty*, and *It Happened One Night*. Born in 1901 in Ohio, he learned to love language and acting at a young age. He started out as a stage actor, then appeared in silent films between 1924 and 1926. By 1932, about the time he started coming to the Yucca Loma, he was starring in Hollywood movies, including *No Man of Her Own*, where he met his co-star, Carole Lombard. They married in 1939, and made several visits to the ranch. When Carole was killed in a plane crash in 1942, he was totally devastated. For awhile he was in seclusion before resuming his visits.

Clark was mechanically inclined, even as a boy; he enjoyed working on cars, hunting, and physical work. When he came to the high desert to stay at either the North Verde Ranch (later the Kemper Campbell Ranch) or the Yucca

Loma, he enjoyed outdoor activities. Historian Ellsworth Sylvester claimed that Gable dug the swimming pool, planted trees, and built a bath house at Yucca Loma. Both ranches reported that he liked to go hunting. In her interview, Mildred DeMott said that one day her son Frank took him out in his Model T to show him how to shoot. Gable saw a rabbit and he yelled, "Frank, stop." Frank stopped so suddenly that Gable flew up against the windshield and knocked out two teeth. (Another account is that they were caps). He had to go to Hollywood right away to replace them. She claims he was a good sport about it, and that he "was a very interesting and very fine man." Jean DeBlasis recalled that Clark always stayed at the Yucca Loma but often visited the North Verde Ranch. Her brother, Kemper, had an ear infection and fever, but although the weather was very cold, their mother, Litta Belle Campbell, let him go rabbit hunting with Clark. When they both returned soaking wet, Litta Belle said she was afraid she was going to have her marriage license revoked (because she had allowed Kemper to go out in bad weather).

A "scandal" that turned out to be true involved the actress Loretta Young. During the filming of *Call of the Wild* in 1935, a steamy affair with Gable resulted in her pregnancy. (See Loretta Young). People in Hollywood suspected the child was his, mostly because of her daughter's large ears, similar to her father's. It wasn't until 1999, when her biographer asked her to confirm the story, that Loretta admitted it was true.

After Carole Lombard's death, Clark joined the U.S. Army Air Force in 1942, where he flew five combat missions, until his plane was hit and one man died and two were injured. When MGM found out, they asked the Air Force to reassign him to non-combat duty. He earned the Distinguished Flying Cross, and before the war was over he was promoted to Major. He was a favorite of Adolf Hitler, who offered a sizeable award to anyone who could capture him and bring him in unscathed.

Clark's last movie was *The Misfits*, co-starring Marilyn Monroe. The film was beset by problems, but completed in 1960. He insisted on doing his own stunts in the movie, although he was fifty-nine years old. He died of a heart attack in November, 1960, before the film was released. Marilyn Monroe died of a drug overdose in August, 1962.[10]

Director Dorothy Arzner, 1927.

Clark Gable with horse circa 1930s.

Bill Holden (1918-1981) - William Holden was only twenty-one when he starred in *Golden Boy* in 1939. Director Rouben Mamoulian brought him to the Yucca Loma shortly after discovering him at the Pasadena Playhouse. He had been looking for some fresh new talent, and when he learned that Bill was an ex-Golden Gloves fighter he decided he was just right for the part. Mamoulian also brought the writers Dan Taradash and Louis Meltzer to the ranch, where they would get plenty of rest and work with him until the script was finished. He coached Bill Holden on each segment of the script. Holden became one of the biggest movie stars of all time, starring in some of the most popular films in Hollywood. Unfortunately, he died from a fall in his apartment when he hit his head, in 1981. He visited the ranch with his wife, Brenda.[11]

Hedda Hopper (1885-1966) - Born in Pennsylvania, Hedda married matinee idol DeWolf Hopper in 1913. They moved to Hollywood, where they both had active movie careers. After a divorce, she appeared in dozens of films; then in 1936 she started a gossipy radio show. But she found her calling when she became a rival of Louella Parsons as a newspaper gossip columnist, a job she held for twenty-eight years. She became known for large flamboyant hats and strong opinions. She was often critical of some of the stars; some say her No. 1 suspect of disdain was Joan Bennett, who mailed Hopper a skunk as a Valentine's Day gift in 1950 with a note that read "You Stink!" In the 1950s, Hedda used her inside information on movie celebrities to aid FBI Director, J. Edgar Hoover in his investigations into their political affiliations, especially if they had any association with the Communist party. Her columns always had good things to say about Rancho Yucca Loma, where she was a frequent guest. Either she kept her opinions to herself when visiting, or perhaps some Hollywood people avoided the ranch when she was there. John Barry recalled that she enjoyed going to the ranches to watch the cowboys brand the cattle, and that she liked to tell funny stories. She raved about the meals prepared by the cook, Nat Joseph, and when Gwen Behr died and the ranch was closing, she hired him to be her own personal cook.[12]

Priscilla Lane (1915-1995) - The youngest of five daughters, Priscilla and two of her sisters had successful singing careers, and later appeared in several films. Priscilla was in over a dozen movies of the 1930s and 1940s. In 1943 she starred in a Jack Benny comedy, *The Meanest Man in the World*. She was a popular visitor to the Yucca Loma Ranch during WWII, where she met John Barry. They were engaged to be married, but in 1942 she met Joseph Howard at one of the other guest ranches, and they were married. A *Daily Press* columnist, Wally Gould, wrote that he got to know the Lane sisters when he saw them every weekend at Yucca Loma Ranch or Kemper Campbell Ranch gatherings. Priscilla's good friend Pat Bergen recalled that the two friends spent a lot of time at the *Victor Press* office. A man had been murdered at the cement plant, possibly for money, and there was much discussion about the clues or suspicions about who had done it. The Sheriff was delighted to have a pretty movie star interested in a local crime. So Priscilla and Pat rode along with the Sheriff to the suspect's house to interview and arrest the suspect. Pat said that the "sirens were blaring and the lights on and the whole enchilada." It was a good story for the local newspapers.[13]

Jesse Lasky (1880-1958) **and Family** - Jesse Lasky was born in San Francisco, where he learned to play the cornet. He and his sister Blanche formed a touring vaudeville act, and he acted in several plays. Blanche married Sam Goldfish, who later changed his name to Goldwyn, and was a founder of MGM. Jesse married Bessie, an accomplished painter, in 1909. His sons both became successful in the movie business. His daughter, Betty, a writer and film historian, has written a book about her father's long career, which included working with Cecil DeMille to produce *The Squaw Man* in 1914, and establishing Paramount Pictures with Adolph Zukor from 1916-1932. He had many ups and downs, and although he had tax problems at the time of his death, Betty said that he always maintained his courage and enthusiasm to the end. He said, "You're never broke if you have an idea." Betty has wonderful memories of her family visiting the ranch, starting in the mid-1930s. Almost every other weekend in the summer the family went to a hotel at Lake Arrowhead, and in the cooler weather they came to Rancho Yucca Loma, which was her favorite. She loved to swim in the pool, although the adults thought the water was too cold. The children liked it because they had more privacy, and were free to do what they wanted. As a teenager, Betty had a crush on John Barry, who was just getting started in the newspaper business.[14]

Beirne Lay (1909-1982) - (See also Sy Bartlett). Beirne Lay enlisted in the U.S. Army in 1932, when he began pilot training. He was flying for the Army Air Corps delivering mail when there were several fatal accidents, causing public criticism. He began writing rebuttal articles and pieces on aviation in general that were published in several magazines. He became managing editor for *The Sportsman Pilot* in 1935, and began writing a book about his experiences in pilot training. He sold film rights to Paramount Pictures, but most of his book was rewritten by editors. After the outbreak of World War II, he returned to duty as a flying instructor. He wrote speeches for the Chief of the Army Air Corps, and in 1942 was made brigadier general. After promotion to lieutenant commander, in 1943 he was granted permission to obtain combat experience. He flew five missions with the 100th Bomb Group, and wrote a detailed critique of the mission, resulting in an article in *The Saturday Evening Post*. In May, 1944, he led his group to France on its fourth combat mission, where some were shot down. He wrote a second book about the experience. After the war he returned to Hollywood, he was approached by Sy Bartlett to write a book, which resulted in *Twelve O'Clock High*. In 1964 the story was aired as a TV series that ran for three years.[15]

Arthur Lubin (1898-1995) - Born in Los Angeles, Arthur worked for theater companies and circuses. In 1922 he decided to become an actor, and worked in Hollywood as well as Broadway. He directed the first Abbott and Costello movie in 1941 and several others, including *Phantom of the Opera* in 1943. But he may have been best known for the *Francis the Talking Mule* series, and the later television series, *Mr. Ed*. Arthur and his dear friend and life partner, Frank Burford, were frequent visitors to the ranch for years, until he purchased a ranch in Lucerne Valley. Once when he came by to visit on his way home from there, he introduced Gwen and the others to a young actor he had just signed on at the studio--Clint Eastwood.[16]

Rouben Mamoulian (1897-1987) - Born in Georgia (under Russia rule), Rouben Mamoulian moved to London to direct plays in 1922, but by 1923 he had moved to New York, where he became head of the School of Drama at the Eastman School of Music in 1925. He directed several shows on Broadway between 1927 and 1949, such as *Porgy and Bess*, *Oklahoma* and *Carousel*. His first film was released in the 1930s, and his last musical, *Silk Stockings*, in 1937. After his involvement in unionizing the Directors Guild of America in 1936, and his continued activity in the union, he became one of the targets of the Hollywood blacklisting in the 1950s. After the Broadway stage production of *Oklahoma* in 1943, Rouben and his wife, Azadia, came to visit the ranch for a couple of months, and returned other summers.[17]

Lewis Meltzer (1911-1995) - Meltzer, a screenwriter, went to Hollywood in 1938 at the request of the director Rouben Mamoulian. He worked at several studios during his thirty-year career, according to his son Joshua. He worked on several films, including *Man with the Golden Arm* in 1955, and *Golden Boy*, along with Dan Taradash, in 1939. The pair came to the quiet hideaway of Yucca Loma to finish the script, where they could work in their room with a thermos of coffee, and sometimes had meals brought in.[18]

Jess Oppenheimer (1913-1988) - A frequent visitor to the ranch, Jess moved to Hollywood in 1936, where he was hired as a comedy writer for Fred Astaire's radio program, and then as a gag writer for Jack Benny. He went on to write comedy for many other variety programs, and sketches for Hollywood stars, such as Fred and Gracie Allen, Marlene Dietrich, Bob Hope, and many others. During World War II he was hired for *The Baby Snooks Show*, starring Fanny Brice. Later he became the head writer, producer, and director for five of the six seasons of the *I Love Lucy* show. John Barry told the story that Jess came to the ranch for a long visit at the advice of experts at the studio and even a psychiatrist, with the purpose of growing back his thick black hair that he had lost. His nickname was "Skinhead" around Hollywood. He was told to sleep on a 1/2" wooden board and seek peace and quiet, with no drinking or partying. But Barry claims that when he came back the next year, "Guess what they still called him?"[19]

Gregory Peck (1916-2003) - Best known for his performance as Atticus Finch in the film *To Kill a Mockingbird*, Gregory Peck was a popular star from the 1940s to the 1960s. He starred in several other popular films over the years. Helen Berger recalled that he and his wife visited the ranch frequently with their two boys. When the boys found a cow's skull on the desert and wanted to keep it, their parents let them keep it on the roof of their ranch house.[20]

Cesar Romero (1907-1994) - Romero was an actor in film, radio, and television for almost sixty years. He played Latin lovers in many films, and the Joker in the *Batman* TV series. He liked to come to the desert to rest and relax. Helen Berger said that he would have his quiet time, then on Saturday night he would go to the Green Spot in Victorville for partying and dancing; by Sunday morning, when it was time to go home, he was exhausted.[21]

Irwin Shaw (1913-1984) - One of the most prolific writers of the twentieth century, Shaw is best known for his 1948 novel, *The Young Lions*, most of which he wrote while visiting the Yucca Loma, according to newspaper accounts and Ann Sudlow's memoir. The book was made into a film starring Marlon Brando in 1958. He wrote twelve novels, including *Beggarman, Thief*, and *Rich Man, Poor Man*, which was the source of a television miniseries. Several of his novels and short stories were the basis of movies. When he and his wife Marian came to visit they lived in Gwen's house. By that time she was ill, and had moved into the front bedroom of the ranch house, organizing the needs and rhythms of the ranch from her bed.[22]

Dan Taradash (1913-2003) - A writer with a background in law, Taradash wrote plays for Broadway before moving to Hollywood, where his first assignment was as one of four writers on the screen version of Clifford Odets' *Golden Boy,* completed in 1939. His frequent visits to the Yucca Loma were to work with Louis Meltzer on the script. He was a successful screenwriter for many more movies, especially *From Here to Eternity.*[23]

Loretta Young (1913-2000) - A visitor to the ranch in 1935 when she was an actress in the movie *Call of the Wild* with Clark Gable, this desert retreat was a possible location of their affair together. Clark Gable was married at the time. When a pregnancy resulted, Loretta took a "vacation" in England, and returned to the United States to her mother's house in Venice to give birth to Judith Young. Judy was transferred to an orphanage outside of Los Angeles, and when she was nineteen months old her grandmother announced to the gossip columnist Louella Parsons that Loretta had adopted the child. The girl's true parentage was widely rumored in entertainment circles, but it wasn't until 1999 that Young finally confessed that Judy was her biological child as a result of a brief affair with Gable. Judy was raised as "Judy Lewis", taking the name of Young's second husband, Tom Lewis.[24]

Fred Zinnemann (1907-1997) - Another favorite at the Yucca Loma was the director Fred Zinnemann. While studying law in his native Vienna, he became interested in film, and traveled to America to pursue his dream. He worked on several films before turning to features, and then B mysteries. His best-known work was *High Noon*, released in 1952. *From Here to Eternity* won eight Academy Awards in 1953. Other notable films included *Oklahoma* and *A Man For All Seasons*. Zinnemann continued work through his eighties, after winning four Academy Awards and directing many major films. Helen Berger wrote that Fred told her that in World War II he was recruited by the FBI to be an undercover agent because he had a photographic memory, but he couldn't tell his family until many years later. John Barry remembered that Zinnemann liked to bring his wife, Rene, and his friend, Gunther, from Vienna, to visit the ranch. Later when he heard that Gwen was dying, Fred left his busy schedule in Hollywood to visit her and show his support.[25]

MORE NAME DROPPING

Helen Berger mentioned that **Cary Grant** (1904-1986) was very well-liked on the ranch. Once he dropped by to make reservations for his ex-wife--she didn't say which one. Singer-Dancer **Ginger Rogers** (1911-1995) was a regular visitor (without Fred Astaire). **Tyrone Power** (1914-1958) and his wife **Annabel** were regular visitors. English actress, **Dame Gladys Cooper** (1888-1971), visited with her daughter. **Olivia De Havilland,** (1916-   ), recipient of two Academy Awards and many other acting awards, was known to visit the ranch. She has lived in Paris since 1960. **Rosalind Russell** (1907-1956) enjoyed the laid-back attitude and Nat's cooking. **Ingrid Bergman** (1915-1982) took riding lessons at Yucca Loma. There were many others.

Character actress Beulah Bondi was a regular guest and dear friend for over twenty years.

Twelve O'Clock High was written at the Yucca Loma by Sy Bartlett and Beirne Lay, Jr. in 1948 as a novel, then as a movie script in 1949. The 1950 film was an instant hit and won two Academy Awards.

Dan Taradash was one of four writers on the screen version of Clifford Odets' 1939 movie *Golden Boy*.

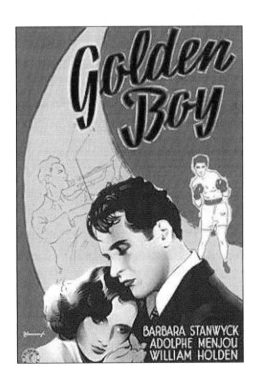

Jesse Lasky's daughter Betty Lasky remembers happy days at the Yucca Loma Ranch.

NOTES

[1] "George Abbott," *The Great Stage Directors* (New York: Facts on File, 1994), 1-4; Ann Rivers Sudlow, unpublished manuscript, July 2001.

[2] "Maude Adams," *Wikipedia* article; Comments by Helen Berger in her 1994 talk to Dr. Lyman's Local History class at Victor Valley College.

[3] "Eddie 'Rochester' Anderson," *Contemporary Black Biography*, Vol. 30 (Farmington Hills, MI: Gale Group, Inc., 2002), 10-12.

[4] "Dorothy Arzner," *International Dictionary of Films & Filmmakers, 2: Directors,* 3rd ed. (Detroit: St. James Press, 1997), 38-39; Helen Berger talk.

[5] "Sy Bartlett," Ephriam Katz: *The Film Encyclopedia* (New York: Thomas Crowell, 1979), 86; Sudlow manuscript.

[6] "Jack Benny," *Current Biography Yearbook 1963* (New York: The H.W. Wilson Company, 1963), 28-30; "Buck Benny Rides Again," *San Bernardino Sun,* November 15, 1939.

[7] "Carrie Jacobs-Bond," *The New Grove Dictionary of Music & Musicians*, 2nd ed. Vol. 3 (London: Macmillan Publishers, Ltd., 2001), 850-51; *Wikipedia* article; Helen Berger talk.

[8] "Beulah Bondi," *Films & Filmmakers, 3: Actors & Actresses*, 3rd ed. (Detroit: St. James Press, 1997), 246; Helen Berger talk; "Beulah Bondi Now at Work on 'Mr. Smith Goes to Washington," *Victor Press*, May 5, 1939.

[9] "Gower & Marge Champion," *Current Biography 1953* (New York: The H.W. Wilson Company, c.1954), 110-112; *Wikipedia*.

[10] "'Clark Gable," *International Dictionary of Film & Filmmakers 3: Actors & Actresses* (Detroit: St. James Press, 1997), 437-440; "All the Household at Yucca Loma Hurried Into Town to see Clark Gable's Splendid Work in Test Pilot," *Victor Press,* May 13, 1938; Interview with Ellsworth Sylvester, 1996; Mildred DeMott transcript of 12/4/70 Interview #4 in VVC Library; Helen Berger talk.

[11] "Bill Holden," *Films & Filmmakers 3: Actors & Actresses (*Detroit: St. James Press, 1997), 551-555.

[12] "Hedda Hopper," *Current Biography 1942* (New York: The H.W. Wilson Company, 1943), 391-392; *Biography for Hedda Ho*pper on Internet.

[13] Wally Gould, "When Lane Loved in the Victor Valley," *Daily Press*, December 5, 1993; Berger.

[14] "Jesse Lasky and family," Phone conversation from Evelyn O'Brien with Jesse Lasky's daughter Betty on August 23, 1997, and subsequent phone calls; "Jesse Lasky," (*Gale Encyclopedia of Biography*, Sept. 16, 1913); Betty Lasky's website @ http://www.jesse-l-lasky.com/BettyLasky.html; Sudlow.

[15] "Bierne Lay, Jr.," *Contemporary Authors*, Vol. 107 (Detroit: Gale Research, 1989), 277; Wikipedia article; Sudlow manuscript, 12.

[16] "Arthur Lubin," *The Film Encyclopedia*, 738-739. Berger.

[17] "Rouben Mamoulian," *The Great Stage Directors*, (New York: Facts on File, 1994), 198-200; Berger; Sudlow.

[18] Lewis Meltzer -- "Golden Boy," M*agill's Survey of Cinema*, First Series, Vol. 2. (Englewood Cliffs, N.J.: Salem Press, 1980), 651-652; Sudlow.

[19] "Jess Oppenheimer," *Contemporary Authors*, Vol. 127, (1989), 328-329; Barry, Rancho Yucca Loma, 25-28.

[20] "Gregory Peck," *The Encyclopedia of Hollywood*, (New York: Facts on File, 1990), 903; Berger.

[21] "Cesar Romero," *The Film Encyclopedia*, 990-991; Barry, 12-14; Berger.

[22] "Irwin Shaw," *Contemporary Authors, New Revision Series Vol. 21*, 758-761; Sudlow,7.

[23] "Daniel Taradash," *International Dictionary of Films and Filmmakers 4: Writers and Production Artists* (Detroit: St. James Press, 1997), 812-813; Sudlow.

[24] "Loretta Young," *The Encyclopedia of Hollywood,* 470-471; Evelyn O'Brien's notes; Wikipedia.

[25] "Fred Zinnemann," *The Encyclopedia of Hollywood*, 473-474; Barry, 60-66.

George Denny, host of America's Town Meeting of the Air, broadcast from
New York City's Town Hall, and wife Jeannie.

WRITERS AND ARTISTS

In addition to the actors, directors, and other creative people from the stage and screen who enjoyed the ranch, artists such as Ramos Martinez, and writers such as Ernest Thompson Seton appreciated the peaceful atmosphere of the ranch and the stimulation of the many other intelligent and accomplished guests they met there.

Edwin Corle (1906-1956) - Edwin Corle wrote many books about the Southwest and Native Americans. He was a big fan of the Yucca Loma; his 1941 book, *Desert Country*, was dedicated to Gwen Behr, and he devoted several pages to the High Desert ranches, Yucca Loma in particular. His section on John Barry and the *Victor Press* was extensive. He said that the newspaper "runs nothing but the local news...A head-on collision at Barstow forty miles away, resulting in two deaths and injury to two others... is of no moment whatsoever to Mr. Barry." He quotes Mr. Barry as saying that "if the President of the United States should suddenly die, he would have to do it within thirty miles of Victorville or the *Press* would not consider the fact worth publishing."[1] Corle visited the ranch with his wife Helen in the 1930s, and later with his second wife Jean.[2]

George Denny (1899-1959) - Ann Rivers Sudlow and Helen Berger both remembered that the Denny family were regular visitors, even though they came all the way from New York. George was the moderator and producer for the America's Town Meeting of the Air, broadcast from New York City's Town Hall from 1935-1951. He wanted to create a program that would replicate the Town Meetings that were held in the early days of the United States. The purpose was to enhance the public's interest in current events, a program that would be entertaining as well as mentally challenging. It featured well-known experts who presented various perspectives on issues of the day. The show became so popular that during the late 1930s and into the early 1940s, Denny was asked to write a column for *Current History* magazine. Editors found it so useful that some of the content was put into booklet form, and sent to public school civics teachers.[3] The conversation around the dinner table must have been lively and stimulating when the Denny family visited.

Will James (1892-1942) - Will James was both an artist and a writer of the American West. Born in Canada, he started drawing at the age of four on the kitchen floor. He wrote many novels and short stories; most of his children's stories were self-illustrated. His story, *Smoky, the Cowhorse*, won the coveted

Newbery medal in 1926.[4]   In the late 1930s he lived at the Godshall C Bar G Ranch on Bear Valley Road. Mr. James wrote at least one book, *Flint Spears*, while living at the Godshall Ranch. He visited, but did not live at the Yucca Loma.[5]

In his memoirs, John Barry tells the story that Mr. James spent a lot of time at the Green Spot bar in Victorville, where his fans would buy him drinks. Sometimes he consented to draw a picture with soap on the long mirror on the back of the bar, which he obtained when he talked the bartender, Lew Parrish, into stealing it from the men's room.   The picture usually "depicted a cowboy riding a bucking horse with a lasso catching a bawling calf around the neck at the mirror's far end." Congratulations and farewell drinks were enjoyed at the end of the evening. Barry said that the next day Lew told him that the owner, John Roy, became incensed when he saw the drawing and threatened to fire Lew if it happened again.   A couple of days later a Rolls Royce pulled up at the curb and the driver shuffled into the bar. He was wearing a white suit and white sombrero, and sporting a diamond ring. After downing a couple drinks, the driver asked, "Ever hear or see some kind of cowboy named Will James?" Lew told him Will was a regular. The stranger smiled and said, "Ever see any of his drawings? Heard over in Vegas he draws on bar mirrors." Lew said, "Many times n ours here." The stranger asked, "Boss ever think to take down a decorated mirror? Save it? Anyone ever snap photographs?" Lew explained that his boss would not allow it. The stranger told him that they were building a multimillion dollar night club in Las Vegas and were willing to pay ten thousand dollars or more for a mirror decorated and signed by Will James. When he told Mr. Roy, the boss said, "If this Will guy comes in again, tell him John Roy wants to talk to him. Tell him drinks and soap or anything else he wants will be free." Lew couldn't laugh.[6]   [This Las Vegas part may or may not be a true story, but according to several other witnesses, he liked to draw on mirrors with soap.]

Ramos Martinez (1871-1946) - Martinez was a struggling young artist in Mexico when he was discovered by the wealthy philanthropist, Phoebe Hearst. Born in 1871 in Monterrey, Mexico, Alfredo Ramos Martinez was awarded a first prize at the age of fourteen at an art exhibition in San Antonio, Texas for his portrait of the governor of the Mexican state of Nuevo Leon. The prize was a scholarship to the national academy of Bellas Artes in Mexico City. His family moved to a town on the outskirts so that he could attend, which he did for eight years. However, he was unhappy with the program and often skipped classes to return to his outdoor sketching of everyday life and open spaces, and his insistence on an "Open Air" approach to painting. Ramos longed to go to Europe, where the Impressionist movement was well-known. In 1899, Phoebe Hearst attended a formal dinner hosted by the Mexican President Porfirio Diaz. Ramos had hand painted menus for the occasion. Mrs. Hearst liked them very much, and asked to meet the artist. She offered him a monthly stipend to study in Paris. He seeped himself in the abundance of art in Europe, where he specialized in painting farmers and day laborers, and women and children.

Once when he ran out of drawing paper the concierge at the inn where he was staying gave him newsprint, which became a favorite medium for Ramos. In 1906, apparently satisfied with the progress of her protégé, Phoebe Hearst informed Ramos that he was now capable of living off his works and withdrew her support.[7]

He returned to Mexico during the Revolution of 1910, which saw the ouster of Porfirio Diaz the following year. He became assistant director of a new "Free Academy," and started the Open Air Schools project, where he taught and expanded the program until 1928. That year he married Maria Sodi Romero, and a

Martinez mural in Gwen Behr's house, 1930s.

year later their daughter, Maria, was born with a congenital bone disease. She became his main preoccupation, and the family moved to Minnesota for treatment at the Mayo Clinic. When the doctors there recom-mended a warmer climate for Maria, the family moved to Los Angeles. After moving to California, Ramos' canvases evolved from what he had been doing to religious imagery featuring Madonna and Child and the Virgin of Guadalupe, primarily because of the passion aroused from the suffering of his infant daughter and his wife.[8]

In the early 1930s, Gwen Behr invited him to stay at the Rancho Yucca Loma for a year, where he painted frescoes in every cabin, as a kind of painted prayer for his daughter. Ann Rivers Sudlow remembers that he did two mural figures, an Aztec man and woman in the ranch house where he was living, and a male figure in Gwennie's house she nicknamed Pancho. Ramos stood small in stature and had arthritis in his wrists, but had a "sweet gentle personality." Many of the paintings done at the ranch were on newsprint, as he had learned in Paris.[9]

Ramos' reputation grew, and he was commissioned to paint murals and exhibit his works throughout California. The Hollywood set discovered him, and he was asked to paint murals and paintings in many of their homes. Some of Martinez' murals are still in existence throughout California. But most of his artwork in the Yucca Loma buildings disappeared when the houses were left unattended before being burned in a fire. Few exist locally. John Barry said that one of the frescoes of the Virgin of Guadalupe with a votive candle at her feet was removed together with sections of brick and stucco walls from the Yucca Loma Ranch. For awhile it was displayed at the Apple Valley Ranchos' office across from the Apple Valley Inn, and can now be found in the Victor Valley Museum.[10] Some of his work can be viewed at the Margaret Fowler Garden at Scripps College in Claremont, where the college commissioned a mural on one wall of the garden in 1946. Ramos outlined the mural and had started on some of the sections when he became ill. He died on November 8, 1946. In 1994 a Getty Endowment grant allowed the mural to be conserved.[11] Many of his works are now sold for thousands, sometimes millions of dollars.

Mary Roberts Rinehart (1876-1958) - According to local historian Ellsworth Sylvester, the writer Mary Roberts Rinehart had a house built at Yucca Loma for herself that had low ceilings and a low doorway because of her small stature (4'11").[12] She liked to come to the ranch to work on her novels. Mary was often called the American Agatha Christie. She was married with three children when the couple lost their savings in the stock market crash of 1903. To earn income, she started writing, and wrote forty-seven short stories in 1927. The *Circular Staircase* was a best seller, and she continued to sell popular novels. She loved to travel and visit parks and dude ranches in Western United States, a subject of several magazine articles and some of her stories.[13]

Tony Sarg (1880-1942) - Tony Sarg, born in 1880, had been raised around puppets he inherited from his grandmother's collection. He was born in Guatemala, and grew up in Germany, then moved to England where he met his wife, and came to the United States. He developed the puppets into a hobby, and was called "America's Puppet Master." In 1921 Sarg animated the cartoon film, *The First Circus*. In 1928 he designed and help build tethered helium-filled balloons up to 125-feet long, resembling animals, for the Macy's annual Thanksgiving Day parade. In 1935 he designed Macy's elaborate animated window display between Thanksgiving and Christmas. Tony passed away in 1942.[14]

Visitors to the Yucca Loma remembered that once when Tony Sarg stayed on the ranch, the roof of one of the buildings was leaking after a heavy rain. The playful Tony stood on a ladder and drew cartoons around the spots, which was a big hit with the other guests. He painted cowboys and Indians on the ceiling and walls of the main house dining room in 1925, and no one ever painted over them. They were there when the house was demolished in the late 1950s.[15]

William Allen White (1868-1944) - William White, the renowned newspaper editor of the *Emporia* (Kansas) *Gazette,* was Catherine Boynton's cousin. White had bought the newspaper in 1895, and the newspaper is still in the White family in 2014. Mr. White also wrote several books on politics, as well as short stories and novels.[16] During the time Rancho Yucca Loma was in existence, he made frequent visits with his family to the ranch. Members of Catherine's family and some of her friends, including Nini Barry and son John, also visited the White family in Kansas. Mr. White was an inspiration and mentor to John Barry, resulting in John's education, experience, and contacts that led up to the purchase of the *Victor Press* in 1937.[17] In Catherine's biography, her cousin Mr. White is quoted from one of his early visits when he was taking his first walk in the desert, "Now that cultivation is almost at your door, you will soon be able to develop your retreat."[18]

Martinez' Madonna from above the fireplace in one of the ranch guest houses--now at the Victor Valley Museum.

Flower Vendors, circa 1940 by Alfredo Ramos Martinez.

1928 illustration from *The Drifting Cowboy* by Will James

One of Tony Sarg's illustrations from a ceiling in one of the guest houses at Yucca Loma.

NOTES

[1] Edwin Corle, *Desert Country* (New York: Duell, Sloan & Pearce, 1941), 219-221.

[2] Ann Rivers Sudlow, *Rancho Yucca Loma*, (unpublished manuscript, 2001), 8.

[3] *Dictionary of American Biography*, Supp. 4: 1946-1950, "Denny, George Vernon, Jr." (New York: Charles Scribner's Son, 1974), 160-161.

[4] *Contemporary Authors*, Vol. 19, "James, William Roderick." (Detroit: Gale Research, 1980), 224-225.

[5] Evelyn O'Brien's notes, n.d.

[6] John Barry, *Rancho Yucca Loma*, (unpublished manuscript, n.d.), 15-20.

[7] Small, George Raphael, *Ramos Martinez: His Life and Art* (Westlake Village, CA: F & J Publishing Corp., 1975). Copy in Victor Valley College Library.

[8] Sudlow, 8.

[9] John Barry, *Ramos Martinez and the Madonna in the Fireplace* (unpublished).

[10] Barry, *Rancho Yucca Loma*, 43-46.

[11] *The Alfredo Ramos Martinez Research Project.* www.alfredoramosmartinez.com/pages.biography.html

[12] Ellsworth Sylvester interview with author, circa 1996

[13] *Contemporary Authors*, Vol. 166, "Rinehart, Mary Roberts," (Detroit: Gale Research, 1962), 331-335.

[14] *Dictionary of American Biography*, Supp. 3, "Sarg, Tony," (New York: Charles Scribner's Sons, 1973), 684-685.

[15] John Barry, *Rancho Yucca Loma*, 37-39

[16] *Dictionary of American Biography*, Vol. 9, Pt. 3, "American Novelists, 1910-1945," "William Allen White" (Detroit: Gale Research, 1981), 142-146.

[17] John Barry, 33-34

[18] Nini Barry, *Catherine Boynton* (unpublished biography found at Victor Valley Museum), 2013.

"For the Rivers kids, the Mojave Desert was endlessly inviting. No one worried about where we were, so some days we rode our horses off to investigate the abandoned homesteader shacks; many still had the 1915 and 1916 insulating newspapers with two-inch high headlines: SHIPS SUNK, LINES BREACHED. These we brought home as trophies. Both Gwen and Mildred loved the sun-colored glass bottles with lead in them which turned purple, so this scrounging around the desert had the youngsters adding to their collections. They spotted rattlesnakes, sidewinders, scorpions, big black harmless tarantulas, pack rats, but left them all alone."- Ann Rivers Sudlow

Ernest Seton's paintings of buildings circa 1919.

Top: Nini's house.

Middle: Fireplace with motto: "Come Ye and Know the Peace of the Desert."

Bottom: Other buildings on ranch.

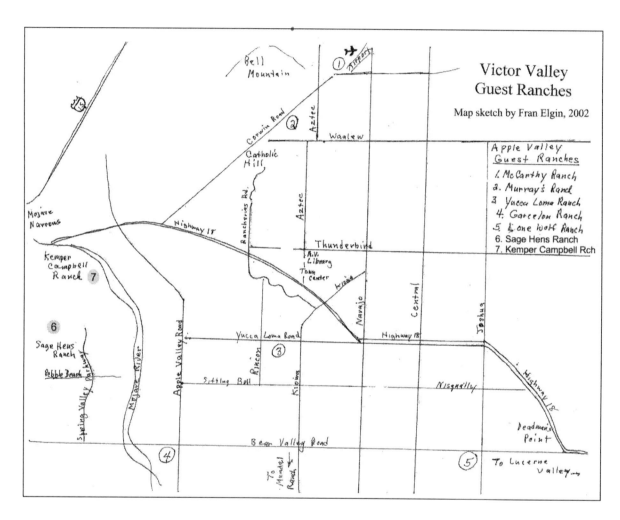

Victor Valley Guest Ranches, map sketch by Fran Elgin 2002.

DUDE OR GUEST RANCHES?

In the 1920s and 1930s, as more and more Americans went to work in the offices and factories of the city, many looked forward to spending their vacations in the wide open spaces. As early as 1841, adventurous men (and a few women) discovered the beauties of the West. In the post-Civil War years, ranchers established the cattle industry of the Great Plains. Visitors came to these ranches to experience the ranch life and to "rough it." At first many of the ranches supplied food and even lodging to the travelers without charge. But as the idea of payment for accommodations to cover some of their expenses became accepted, dude ranching eventually developed. Some came to fish or hunt, and the hosts led pack trips. Others came to experience what it would be like to be a cowboy, and experience cattle drives.[1] Theodore Roosevelt came to the Dakota Territory to visit and ended up starting his own ranch.[2] Montana, Colorado, and Wyoming were popular destinations, especially those close to the mountainous areas. After Yellowstone National Park was created in 1872, people flocked to the ranches nearby.

After the turn of the century there was a "return to nature" movement as people realized that the old West culture was disappearing. Groups developed to support conservation, national parks, and preservation of the wilderness. By 1914, dude ranching in the West was firmly established.[3] The popular writer, Mary Roberts Rinehart, was one of many women who came from the East and took several vacations on the dude ranches. The following is from her book, *Through Glacier Park*:

> *If you are normal and philosophical; if you love your country; if you like bacon, or will eat it anyhow; if you are willing to learn how little you count in the eternal scheme of things; if you are prepared, for the first day or two, to be able to locate every muscle in your body and a few extra ones that seem to have crept in and are crowding, go ride in the Rocky Mountains and save your soul.*[4]

One definition of dude ranches is that they "usually are the year-round homes of the owners rather than temporary dwellings during the tourist season. They offer rooms and meals and have horses available for their guests." Travel by automobile had increased by the 1920s, and roads were improved. Before then, railroads had played an important part in dude ranching. Many railroads started to publish brochures advertising the ranches as destinations. By 1929 the dude ranching industry spread, and ranches sprung up in California, Arizona and other western states.[5]

Although many ranches still attracted people who wanted to get the experience of an actual working ranch (a dude ranch), many were looking for a place to get away from the city life, a place to relax; thus the term "guest ranch" became more popular. However, many offered both to their guests. In the Victor Valley, almost all of them provided horses for riding, and most had tennis courts and swimming pools. Clark Gable, a frequent visitor to the Yucca Loma as well as the North Verde Ranch (Kemper Campbell Ranch), liked to go hunting for rabbits, but, according to local sources, he liked to get his hands dirty by working at the Yucca Loma Ranch.[6] He was the exception, however; most visitors thought of themselves as "guests" rather than "dudes."

By the mid-1920s, Rancho Yucca Loma had evolved from a sanatorium for secretaries, nurses or others who came to recuperate or who needed the services of the founders Dr. Boynton, Dr. Evans, or Dr. Thayer, to a destination where writers could come to write, and actors, directors, artists and other creative people could escape from the pressures of their professional lives. This was the peak time of interest in the idea of dude/guest ranches, and the word spread--especially in Hollywood. Because of Gwen Behr's many contacts with the elite society during her time in New York, and the popularity of train travel, visitors from back East were regular guests, as well as some from Europe. There was an airstrip close to the ranch as there were still plenty of wide-open spaces in the Victor Valley.

Writer Mary Roberts Rinehart. Mary was often called the American Agatha Christie.

94

Ann and Bunny Rivers.

NOTES

[1] "Romance, Rest & Recreation,"
http://www.lib.virginia.edu/etd/theses/ArtsSci/English/1998/Zimmerman).

[2] David McCullough, *Mornings on Horseback* (New York: Simon & Schuster, c1981.) President Theodore Roosevelt, who had craved the out of doors, and "spent many of his earlier years ranching, hunting. birding, and exploring in the American West, increased the size of the national forests, established five national parks, sixteen national monuments,"…and " made conservation a national cause."

[3] Thomas Lesure, "Dude Ranching…the Western Vacation Few Westerners Ever Take," *Desert Magazine*, December, 1960, 26-28.

[4] Mary Roberts Rinehart, *Through Glacier Park* (Boston: Houghton Mifflin Co., 1916). Available online.

[5] Lawrence R. Borne, "Dude Ranching and the Development of the West," *Journal of the West*, July 1978, 83-84.

[6] Clark Gable was mentioned in comments by Ellsworth Sylvester and Jean DeBlasis.

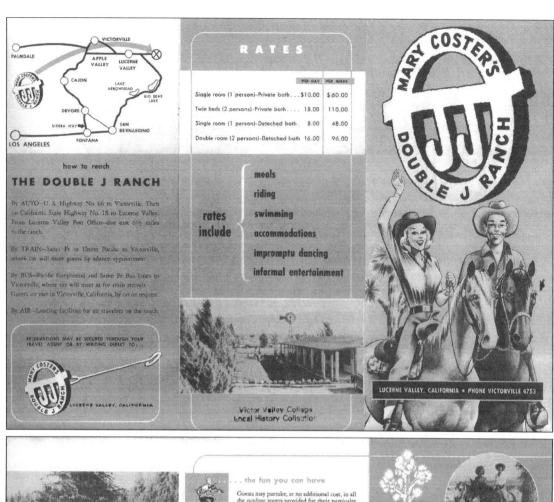

Brochure describing Mary Coster's 1950s Double J Ranch in Lucerne Valley.

VICTOR VALLEY REST HOMES AND GUEST RANCHES

A 1940 brochure touting points of interest in the Victor Valley emphasized the many popular guest ranches in the high desert.[1] In a 1949 flyer, the Victorville Chamber of Commerce declared that the Victor Valley was the "Dude and Guest Ranch Capitol of America." In his 2008 *San Bernardino Sun* column, "Dude, Where's My Ranch?," historian Mark Landis explained that in the 1930s and 1940s these ranches were a mainstay of the High Desert economy, partly due to the fact that the Victor Valley was close enough to be accessible, but still remote enough to deliver the feel of the untamed West. By the 1960s, easy access to Las Vegas and Palm Springs drew vacationers away from the rustic desert ranches to the more sophisticated resorts.[2] Improved roads and more reliable automobile travel may have also contributed to the decline of guest ranch activity here. Some of the ranches, such as the Yucca Loma and the Garcelon Ranch, started out as rest homes and evolved into what were known as guest ranches.

C Bar H Ranch (Lucerne Valley): One of the Lucerne Valley guest ranches was Mary Coster's C Bar H. If movie people or others really wanted to get away to the desert, they drove the extra miles to this even more remote ranch. On a trip to Alaska in the 1990s this author met two ladies who both shared their fond memories of going to the C Bar H in the 1940s.[3]

El Hoco: Corwin Ranch was homesteaded in 1909 by Elmore and Harriet Corwin in the Bell Mountain District close to the present Apple Valley Airport. They called their ranch "El Hoco" to represent their names. In 1925 Harriet opened a rest home that was in existence for about the next ten years. A sign on what is today's Highway 18 announced, "Mother Corwin Rest Home, 5 3/4 Mi." Guests seeking the dry air of the desert stayed in their small cottages for a few days or up to several weeks.[4]

Garcelon Ranch: Between 1900 and 1930 Dr. Frank Garcelon, his son Dr. Harris Garcelon, and their wives homesteaded on property on the east side of the river south of Bear Valley Road and Apple Valley Roads. They made an attempt at growing alfalfa and other crops, including raising turkeys, but that aspect of the ranch was not the major part of their plans. The doctor built the first hospital in the Victor Valley on the ranch and spent most of his time on his medical practice, where he treated shell shock cases after the war. He put some of the men to work shocking hay and other chores. He also hosted such notables as William S. Hart on his guest ranch. During the Prohibition era it was said that some of the best moonshine in the valley was available at the ranch. In 1930 Dr. Garcelon opened a practice in San Bernardino. In 1932 when he was struggling to keep his ranch going during the Depression, his nephew, Stoddard Garcelon Jess, fresh out of three years at UCLA, and looking for something he could do with his hands, purchased the ranch and its debts. He managed to bring it back, and over the next fifty years Jess developed one of the most successful turkey ranch operations in the United States. Several years after his retirement, the ranch became a senior living community, named Jess Ranch.[5]

Godshall Ranch: The Godshall Ranch was located on Bear Valley Road across from Deep Creek Road. *Los Angeles Examiner* manager Max F. Ihmsen established an estate in Apple Valley that grew apples, peaches, alfalfa and turkeys during the 1920s. In 1922 his daughter Josephine married Cal Godshall, and when Mr. Ihmsen died Cal and Josephine inherited the ranch. Godshall introduced the first non-professional amateur rodeo, held at Santa Fe Park in Victorville in 1935. The rodeo was a huge success, and opening day attracted over 6,000 people, including many celebrities. Every year a new queen was selected. Jeanne Godshall was the first, and Anna Lou Rivers, from the Yucca Loma Ranch, was the second. After the Victorville rodeo was dissolved, Jeanne Godshall and her father promoted the first inter-collegian rodeo, which was held on the Godshall Ranch, and also drew big crowds to the rodeo and to the neighboring guest ranches.[6]

Kemper Campbell Ranch (Rancho Verde): Rancho Verde, a cattle ranch on the west side of the river between Bear Valley Road and Highway 18 that dated back to before 1900, was purchased by Kemper Campbell, Sr. and his wife, Litta Belle. In 1924, both were lawyers from Los Angeles. The ranch was split between a man named Sorenson and the Campbells. In 1933 the Campbells opened it as a guest ranch, while continuing the ranching operation. After Kemper Campbell, Jr. died in a plane crash during World War II, the name of the ranch was changed from the North Verde Ranch to Kemper Campbell Ranch to honor their son. In 1940, one famous screenwriter with a drinking problem, Herman Mankiewicz, was sent to the ranch by Orson Welles when he was working on the script for the movie *Citizen Kane* because Welles knew that Mrs. Campbell could keep Mr. Mankiewicz sober as she allowed no alcohol. Many other famous people, including movie stars, visited the ranch, as well as family and old friends, until the guest ranch business closed in 1975. The ranch still exists in the Mojave Narrows, and the guest houses are now permanent residences for several people.[7]

98

Lone Wolf Colony: In 1922 a man named Sam Caldwell and other telephone company employees started a movement to establish a health ranch where veterans returning from World War I, suffering from the effects of poison gas or other injuries, could convalesce. In 1926 the ranch moved to its present location on Bear Valley Road. The year 2014 finds the non-profit ranch still fulfilling its original mission, with a recuperative health facility of ten cabins. In order to increase revenue, they now have an RV Park open to the public.[8]

McCarthy's Guest Ranch (Apple Valley): George and Irene McCarthy came to the Victor Valley in the 1920s and operated the Stewart Hotel in Victorville. Many years later, in 1933, they established their guest ranch in Apple Valley on property now occupied by the Apple Valley Airport. The ranch covered sixty-three acres and included thirteen buildings, housing as many as sixty guests. An advertisement in a Union Pacific brochure on dude ranches claimed that, in addition to horseback riding and swimming, the ranch offered the popular sport of chasing jackrabbits with greyhounds and whippets by auto. When the movie "G.I. Joe" was filmed in the area, Robert Mitchum stayed at the ranch for a week. Another time, Gene Autry and the Tumbling Tumbleweeds stayed there.[9]

Mac's Ranch: After George and Irene McCarthy divorced, the popular George opened up his own ranch up Sky High Road on the eastern end of Apple Valley. His motto was, "Everything free any day the sun does not shine." His brochure offered shuffleboards, horseshoes, and ping-pong. But he claimed that horseback riding was the most popular.[10]

Mendel Ranch: In 1945, Peg and Albert Mendel opened the Circle M Ranch as a guest ranch. Back in 1939, Florence Mendel and her son Albert had purchased 3,000 acres on Tussing Ranch Road between Central and Navajo in Apple Valley. Previous ranchers in the same area included General Mariana, Arthur Hull, and Wiley Tussing. Albert and his first wife, Bernice, bred purebred white-face cattle on 15,000 acres. Albert's second wife, Peg Mendel, recalled that in the guest ranch days the people from other ranches would get together for square dances and other social events. After the guest ranch closed in 1954, they established the Golden Land Printing Company, which successfully printed brochures, yearbooks, and other publications for many years.[11]

Murray's Overall Wearing Dude Ranch: Touted as the only African-American dude ranch in the world, the ranch started after Nolie and Lela Murray bought the 400-acre ranch from Arthur "Abe" Cook in 1926 for $100. The ranch was at Waalew Road and what is now Dale Evans Parkway. In the early days Murray's was a place for troubled kids, black and white, who were sent to the ranch by the courts. During the 1930s and 1940s when dude ranches became popular, the word spread, and *Life Magazine* featured an article with photos of the children, as well as movie people who came to the ranch. In the 1930s, Herb Jeffries, a vocalist who had performed with the Duke Ellington Orchestra, made several singing black cowboy movies at the Murray Ranch. (Mr. Jeffries came to Apple Valley in October, 2013 to attend a celebration of his 100th birthday.) The famous boxer, Joe Louis, trained at the ranch, and other well-known celebrities came to the desert to swim, play tennis, ride horses, and play baseball. Lena Horne, Bill "Bojangles" Robinson, the Four Tones, and others enjoyed the hospitality. Visitors from other ranches were welcomed, and Murray's visitors were known to visit the Yucca Loma and other nearby ranches. The singer-actress Pearl Bailey bought the ranch in 1955, but was only there a few years.[12]

Sagehens Ranch: In 1936, Lily Ann Phillips, a widow, and two friends, both lawyers, visited the North Verde Guest Ranch in Victorville (now Kemper Campbell Ranch). Their good friend, Litta Belle Campbell, suggested that if they start a guest ranch, she could send her overflow to them. They found 120 acres 3 1/2 miles to the south with a house and garage on a hilltop by the golf course on what is now Spring Valley Lake. In 1937 Lily's friends Winnie and Florence went in with her, and they called their venture the Sage Hen Guest Ranch, but shortened it to Sagehens Ranch. During World War II Lily Ann and others in the ranch family took turns sitting in a small shack on a desert rise watching for enemy planes. On the wall was a poster with silhouettes of war planes, both friendly and enemy. No one ever spotted anything except the training planes from the base, and an occasional transport. The ranch became a family adventure that flourished until 1979. By then they were surrounded by Spring Valley Lake, and some of them had failing health.[13]

Sky-Hi Ranch: Another get-away was the Sky-Hi Ranch, on Sky-Hi Ranch Road, high above Highway 18 between Apple Valley and Lucerne Valley. The owner, Mabel Parks, was friends with Litta Belle Campbell and the Sage Hens at Sagehens Ranch.[14]

Winkler Guest Ranch: Winifred Boynton, married to Arthur Winkler, was related to Catherine Boynton through Catherine's first marriage to Frank Boynton. Winifred and Arthur bought forty acres of the Phillips Ranch in Apple Valley, where they operated the Winkler Guest Ranch from approximately 1927-1940. The Winklers had two daughters--Frances and Vera. Frances married Stoddard Jess, and they had two children, Winifred [Wini] and Stoddard Jess, Jr. [Todd]. The Winkler Ranch was merged into the Jess Ranch in the 1940s, and Stoddard Jess donated the property where the Victor Valley Museum stands today. Wini Jess (now married to Gary Ledford) was given a blanket from Rancho Yucca Loma by her grandmother, with Catherine Boynton's name embroidered on it.[15]

During shooting of the movie, "The Great Lie" at the Sagehens Ranch in 1940, actresses Bette Davis and Mary Astor posed with the ranch owners for a memorable photo: (left to right: Helen Phillips, Bette Davis, Lily Phillips, Mary Astor, and Harriet Ann Phillips).

Jean DeBlasis of the Kemper Campbell Ranch, where she lived from when she was a little girl until she died in 2012. Her daughter Celeste, who preceded her in death, wrote a history of the ranch and the family in the book, *Graveyard Peaches*, 1991.

Lela Murray and her husband Nolie operated the famous Overall Wearing Dude Ranch. The Murray's Ranch was in operation for about 30 years.

George McCarthy was the popular manager of Mac Dude Ranch.

Telephone workers clearing land for construction of the Lone Wolf Colony in 1926.

The text within the advertisement/poster image reads:

Irene **McCARTHY'S GUEST RANCH**

OPEN THE YEAR AROUND

ON THE MOJAVE DESERT VICTORVILLE

ON THE MOJAVE DESERT VICTORVILLE

IRENE MC CARTHY'S GUEST RANCH
Victorville, California
RATES- Effective July 1,1949
(Subject to change without notice)

Rates include: room,males,riding,
swimming, all ranch activities.

Daily   Weekly

Room with connecting
bath,each person $9.00 $55.00

Room with private
bath,each person $10.00 $60.00

Modern Stucco Cottages,
bath, each person, $12.00 $75.00

Bunkhouse,
Each person $ 8.00 $50.00

Children 2 to 7 yrs. $5.00 day
Infants up to 2 yrs. $3.00 day
(Monthly rates on application)
7/1/49

McCarthy Guest Ranch on the site where Apple Valley Airport is now located.

McCARTHY'S GUEST RANCH

LOCATION:

McCARTHY'S GUEST RANCH has been operating for over 15 years and is truly an oasis, surrounded by cool green fields and beautiful shade trees on the edge of the Mojave Desert with an abundance of pure deep well water. It lies adjacent to the famous Apple Valley on the south, with the protecting San Bernardino Mountains rising thousands of feet in the distance. The Ranch is just seven miles north east of the thriving town of Victorville, which blends the past with the present modern suburban city life.

CLIMATE:

At an altitude of 3,000 ft. with sunshine practically every day of the year, Summer days are never too warm for comfort and evenings are always cool. FOG & HUMIDITY are unknown, making it an ideal year around climate, and pronounced as one of the most healthful places in the world by famous Doctors.

FOOD:

Food is important and pride is taken in the abundance of wholesome well cooked food, with a large variety of fresh meats and vegetables, served family style. As the McCARTHY GUEST RANCH is also a "Working Ranch" all poultry, eggs, milk, butter, cream, cottage cheese, etc., are produced on the Ranch.

ACTIVITIES:

Horseback riding for which there is no extra charge

is one of the main activities, and there is a fine string of well trained horses for every degree of riding ability, so choose the one that suits you best. BOX STALLS for PRIVATELY OWNED HORSES are available, so bring your own favorite horse if you wish. Guests are permitted to ride either alone or in groups. There are brisk early morning breakfast rides or just a lazy canter over the desert at mid day. Then there are night rides to some rendezvous ending at a steak fry over an open campfire, or rides under the magic spell of a desert moon.

A large sheltered swimming pool with its fresh running water is a major attraction, popular with young and old alike, with its spacious sun deck for sun bathing. There are many more diversified activities on the Ranch, such as Square Dances under the stars; Badminton; Ping Pong; Hiking; Hay rides; Horseshoe Pitching; Hunting; Target Shooting. Guests may help with the regular Ranch chores, feeding, milking, etc., if they wish; or maybe, best of all just sit, rest, relax and enjoy the most wonderful Desert Climate in the World.

ACCOMMODATIONS:

Accommodations are limited to about fifty guests. Rooms being located both in the main Ranch House, and in modern cool shaded cottages. All rooms have outside entrances, private or connecting baths, cross ventilation, comfortable beds with innerspring mattresses; individual heating units for cool evenings.

Photos by Ellie Foote

105

WHAT TO WEAR:

Dress at the Ranch is very informal, comfortable sport cloths, bathing suits, sun suits, sweaters and leather coats for cool evenings. Of course big hats, bluejeans or frontier pants and cowboy boots, are always appropriate for western riding in the desert country.

MOTOR TRIPS:

There are many close by points of interest easily reached by motor; Famous old Ghost towns, such as Calico; abandoned old mines; mile high mountain lakes, which offer both summer and winter sports; local Rodeos and Country Dances in neighboring Desert towns. Big Bear Lake is one hour by car where one can enjoy all kinds of winter sports.

HOW TO REACH Irene McCARTHY'S GUEST RANCH:

By Automobile:

U. S. Highway 66 to Victorville, then turn east on the State Highway 18, via Mojave River bridge, to a point approximately 2 miles beyond Victorville. Turn LEFT on dirt road at the McCARTHY RANCH sign and continue for five miles to Ranch.

By Train:

From San Francisco and the North take Southern Pacific to Los Angeles; and from Los Angeles take Union Pacific or Santa Fe to Victorville. From the east, Union Pacific or Santa Fe directly to Victorville. Southern Pacific changes at Colton for Victorville.

By Plane:

United Air Lines: T. W. A. & Western Air Lines, or American Airlines to Los Angeles, then Union Pacific or Santa Fe Rail to Victorville. Chartered planes from Oakland to Apple Valley in 3 hours.

Private Planes:

2600 ft. air strip adjacent to Ranch.

By Bus:

Pacific Greyhound and Santa Fe Trailways to Victorville: Ranch car will meet guests by definite appointment at Victorville; or you may take a reasonably priced taxicab to Ranch.

For the Vacation of Your Life and for the Rest of Your Life make McCARTHY'S GUEST RANCH a MUST on your list. **ASK SOME ONE WHO'S BEEN HERE!**

Irene McCARTHY'S GUEST RANCH

Irene McCarthy, Managing Owner

Post Office Box 656, Victorville, Calif.
Telegraph address Western Union, Victorville
Phone Victorville 5211

Member Victorville Dude & Guest Ranch Ass'n
and Hotel Greeters of America

Or see your FAVORITE TRAVEL AGENT

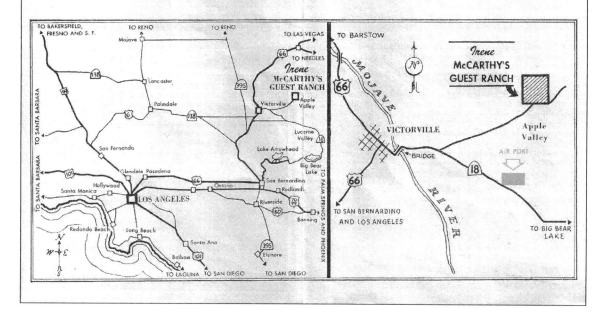

"I remember some socialite Pasadena people coming to the ranch, but they weren't comfortable with the unplanned, laid-back atmosphere of the Yucca Loma." - Ann Rivers Sudlow

[1] Brochure: "Victor Valley, the All Year Desert Resort," 1940; Brochure: Victor Valley Chamber of Commerce, Victorville, 1949.

[2] Mark Landis, "Dude, Where's My Ranch?," *San Bernardino Sun*, June 17, 2008.

[3] Brochure for C Bar H Ranch advertises riding, hiking, dancing, swimming, horseshoes, badminton, ping pong and hunting. $16 daily for two persons with private bath, circa 1940. No extra charge for horses.

[4] Richard D. Thompson, *Elmore and Harriet Corwin and the Corwin Ranch* (Apple Valley, CA: Desert Knolls Press, 2002).

[5] Garcelon Ranch: Stoddard Jess interview; Gary Ledford email, July 2013.

[6] Godshall Ranch: Sudlow manuscript, 8.

[7] Jean DeBlasis, *A Brief History of the [Kemper Campbell] Ranch*. n.d.

[8] "Lone Wolf Colony: A Place to Get Well," *Daily Press*, May 22, 1968.

[9] Bob Jacobs, "Planes May Hum Again Over Old Guest Ranch," *Daily Press*, June 15, 1969.

[10] Brochure: "Mac Dude Ranch;" A *Daily Press* article in 1949 reported that George finally paid on his long-standing bet when a severe storm brought fog, and Mac lost over $100 to people who took him up on the bet.

[11] "Albert Mendel," Two-page history, circa 1985 or 1986.

[12] Richard D. Thompson, *Murray's Ranch: Apple Valley's African-American Dude Ranch* (Apple Valley, CA: Desert Knolls Press, 2002).

[13] William Couey, "Sage Hens Ranch: The Place is Still There, But the Good Times are Gone," *Daily Press*, February 22, 1985; Couey, "Sage Hens Ranch Meets Quick End" *Daily Press*, January 16, 1987.

[14] Sky-Hi Ranch brochure.

[15] Winkler Ranch: Email Correspondence with Gary Ledford in July, 2013.

Note: Other guest ranches in the valley included the **Deep Creek Hacienda**, **Desert Hills**, **El Rancho Verona**, and **Hesperia Dude Ranch**. For more information on the above ranches, see the "Ranches, Guest" files in the Local History collection at Victor Valley College.

Founders of Yucca Loma in 1911: From left-Katharine Evans,
Catherine Boynton, Mildred Strong Rivers and her daughter, Ann Rivers.

VICTOR VALLEY WOMEN IN EARLY 1900s

By the turn of the twentieth century, women in the United States had been petitioning for various rights for years. When Abraham Lincoln opened up homesteading opportunities for all races and all genders, many smart women began filing claims. They also wanted the privilege to vote, and after a lively campaign of speeches, writing, and door-to-door contacts, California became one of the first states to allow suffrage for women in 1911. It seems that Victor Valley women must have felt emboldened to have a say in the development of their community. In 1912 and 1913, several women from Sunrise Valley (now Adelanto) started a literary magazine called *Kingdom of the Sun* that featured local families, ranches, and quality photographs and journalism. One of the editors, **Dr. Henrietta Sweet** from Lucerne Valley, a highly respected doctor, also edited editions of the local newspaper and participated in many Victor Valley activities.[1] Local historians credit **Ursula Poates** as a real estate developer and promoter of Apple Valley land. Her family was among the earliest homesteaders of several tracts of land in Apple Valley.[2] **Mrs. E.M. Potts** had come to Oro Grande with her husband in the early 1900s to establish the Golden State Portland Cement Company. After her husband's death, Mrs. Potts worked hard to fill the void, made sure everyone was paid, and continued to make it a success.[3]

Most of the homesteader women who moved to the Victor Valley about that time were tough, or at least learned to be from the many hardships most of them endured. **Carrie Story** was born in slavery.[4] She and her daughter moved to Bell Mountain from Alabama in 1912, where she homesteaded 160 acres, and eventually bought three houses in Victorville. Carrie earned her living by doing white people's laundry. She was well-known in town; she was tall and carried baskets of laundry and sometimes watermelons on her head. Carrie became famous with the Hollywood set as a fortune teller. Native American **Maria Chapule**, who was born in the 1860s, was well-known in Victorville as a basket maker. Maria lived to be 100 years old--or perhaps older.[5] **Hazel White**, who moved to a ranch near El Mirage Lake in 1914, raised two girls, but she delivered mail, as well as food and supplies to families in the El Mirage/Oro Grande area. Later she was postmaster of the Oro Grande Post Office, and was appointed a Deputy Sheriff.[6] In 1925, **Gertrude Bowen**, along with her husband and children, drove from Los Angeles in their old Model T truck, put up two tents--one for cooking and one for sleeping, and started building a house on their homesteading claim. They built a road up to the ranch, and then one down to Deep Creek.[7] Also in the 1920s, **Litta Belle**

Campbell, an attorney from Los Angeles, and her attorney husband and two children, moved to a ranch at the Mojave Narrows (now the Kemper Campbell Ranch).[8]

When **Dr. Katharine Evans**, **Dr. Catherine Boynton** and her daughter **Gwen**, and their friend **Mildred Strong** founded the Rancho Yucca Loma, they were definitely counted among these creative, intrepid pioneers of the early twentieth Century.

From the 1913 edition of *Kingdom of the Sun.*

Marching for the right to vote 1908 in Oakland, California.

110

Carrie Story (1858-1938)

Maria Chapule (circa 1860-1960). Photo at right is in the early 1890s.

Catherine Boynton
"The Healing Woman."

Gwen Behr, Catherine Boynton's daughter, was hostess of Yucca Loma and community activist until her death in 1954.

Ursula Poates, early Apple Valley pioneer, was featured in the *Kingdom of the Sun* in 1913.

Mrs. E.M. Potts was featured in the 1913 *Kingdom of the Sun.* She died April 28, 1913.

Dr. Henrietta Sweet from Lucerne Valley, editor of *Kingdom of the Sun*.

Gertie Bowen homesteaded with her family in Apple Valley in 1925.

Los Angeles attorneys Litta Belle Campbell and her husband moved to the North Verde Ranch with their children full time in 1931. After their son, Kemper Campbell, died in a plane crash in World War II, they changed the name of the ranch to honor him.

NOTES

[1] *Kingdom of the Sun*, (Sunrise Valley [Adelanto], 1912). Dr. Sweet was an editor in this short-lived but excellent publication "For Women--By Women--To Women" that included profiles of prominent local men and women from 1912-1913. It also featured literary pieces and quality photographs.

[2] *San Bernardino Sun*, May 16, 1911; Edward Leo Lyman , *History of Victor Valley* (Mohahve Historical Society, 2010), 116, 146, 150.

[3] *Kingdom of the Sun*, (1913).

[4] "An Interview with Mrs. Eleanor Washington," *Mohahve* (Victorville: Victor Valley College, 1963), 23-25.

[5] "Maria Chapule dead at 104," *Daily Press*, July 14, 1966.

[6] Hazel White, Transcript of May 1971 Interview #24 in VVC Library.

[7] "Pioneer Woman," *Daily Press*, May 3, 1985.

[8] "Jean DeBlasis talk to Local History Class, Victor Valley College, September 6, 1991.

For use in
HOMESTEAD,
DESERT LAND, and
TIMBER or STONE
Entries.

JJD.

4—348 b   025943

NOTICE FOR PUBLICATION.
(PUBLISHER.)

DEPARTMENT OF THE INTERIOR,

U. S. LAND OFFICE at _Los Angeles Cal.,_

October 25th, 1916, 191

NOTICE is hereby given that _Katharine Evans_ , of

Victorville, Cal., , who, on _February 27th_, 191 6 , made

homestead entry , No. _025943_ , for

SW¼NW¼ Sec.29,E½NE¼ and NE¼SE¼ , Section _30_ ,

Township _5 N.,_ , Range _3 West,_ _S.B._ Meridian,

has filed notice of intention to make _Commutation_

(If homestead, insert "five year," "three year," or "commutation," as case may be.)

Proof, to establish claim to the land above described, before

the _Register and Receiver of U.S.Land Office_ , at

(Name of Officer.)

Los Angeles, Cal., , on the _15th_ day of

December, , 1916, at 9 o'clock A.M.

Claimant names as witnesses:

Harris Garcelon , of

William Addison Foster , of _All_
                                        _of_
Alfred M.Byron , of _Victorville,_

Mrs.William Addison Foster , of _Cal._

Non-Coal.

Nov 3- Dec 1

JOHN D. ROCHE
Register.

News Herald, at Victorville, Cal.
No withdrawals.

Publisher: Return this form to the
Register at the end of the period of publication, with the "Affidavit of Publication"
properly executed.

AFFIDAVIT OF PUBLICATION.

I, _Geo. R. Wickham,_

Manager Legal Advertising, , of the

(Publisher or foreman.)

Victor Valley News-Herald,

(Name of newspaper.)

published _weekly_ at _Victorville,Cal._

(Daily or weekly.)   (Place.)

do solemnly swear that a copy of the above notice, as per clipping

attached, was published _weekly_ in the regular and

(Daily or weekly.)

entire issue of said newspaper, and not in any supplement thereof,

for _five_ consecutive _issues_ , commencing with the

issue dated _Nov.3_ , 1916 , and ending with the

issue dated _Dec. 1_ , 1916

Geo R Wickham

(Signature.)

Subscribed and sworn to before me this _11th_ day of _December_, 1916

John D Roche,

Register.

(Official designation.)

6—3051

The Notice for Publication of homestead application by Katherine Evans posted in the *Victor Valley News-Herald*, 1916. From the National Archives and Records Administration, Washington, DC.

OTHER EARLY SETTLERS & HOMESTEADERS

Homestead laws allowed American citizens over twenty-one to make a desert claim for land available through the government. Although homesteading had been available since 1862, it wasn't until the two decades after 1900 that most claims were made in the Victor Valley. Teddy Roosevelt helped to abolish fraud in the Homesteading Act, which allowed small subsistent farmers get a small plot of land on which to grow some food.[1]

The law stated that a U.S. citizen (or person intending to become one) who was head of a family and over twenty-one years old could qualify for a land grant of 160 acres. To qualify, applicants had to pay a $10.00 registration fee, live on the site for at least six months of every year for five years, and cultivate and improve the land for five full years. Land could be purchased outright by settlers who lived on the land at $1.25 per acre. By 1900, nearly 400,000 individuals or families had filed for land under the provisions of the Act.

Before passage of the Homestead Act, it was nearly impossible for middle or lower class women to acquire land. They had few opportunities for employment, and consequently little ability to accumulate the money for purchasing land. Under the Homestead Act, however, unmarried, widowed or divorced women could claim homestead land as head of a household.[2]

The *Victor Valley News-Herald* published numerous homestead entry notices each week. Associated with homesteading, well-drilling became a thriving business. In 1913 an Apple Valley rancher, Arthur Hull, organized the businessmen in the valley and started the Victor Valley Chamber of Commerce, which by 1917, was already breaking into splinter groups that vied for government money and water rights.

East of the Mojave River, in the area now known as Apple Valley, the word was getting out that there was little land left for homesteading. Those who were paying attention began to flock to the desert. Even before the turn of the century, Ursula Poates was a real estate developer who, along with her husband and three children, were the earliest homesteaders of several tracts of land in Apple Valley. She has been credited with possibly coming up with the name, "Apple Valley." Clayton Cory came in 1902, and William Foster in 1903. At the time there were no schools, churches, doctors, or public utilities or services. John Carroll and Harvey Shaw chose homesteads just south of

Fremont Road (now Del Oro) after it crossed the river. The Cardens grew crops and had cattle and chickens. In 1904 Ed Gilmore took land east of present Apple Valley Road, and McPherson found a spot at the corner of present Bear Valley Road and Deep Creek in 1908. Abbott Phillips settled just west of Deep Creek Road. The Westphal family donated the corner of their property at Bear Valley Road and Deep Creek for the first actual schoolhouse in 1912. Part of the foundation can still be found there today.

In south Apple Valley, Dr. Harris Garcelon settled on the land now occupied by the present Jess Ranch. Max Ihmsen settled on land north of Bear Valley and Deep Creek. Charles TenEyck, and Arthur Hull also homesteaded in 1911. The Hull's ranch was at Kiowa and Tussing Ranch Road. Gus Lintner later installed many of the pumps for irrigating Apple Valley's dry acres. William Hitchcock and William Hunt arrived in 1912. G.C. Lewis found a location for turkeys near the river, and Hitchcock located at Highway 18 and what is now Navajo. Bonadiman's family came in 1914, and Norman Marsh's homestead on the north side of Rock Springs Road was the largest homestead in Apple Valley. Wiley Tussing settled at the corner of Tussing Ranch Road and Central in Section 10.

In north Apple Valley Elmore Corwin and his son George settled near the present Apple Valley Airport in 1908. In the Bell Mountain area were homesteaders William Bronson and Carrie Story in 1911. The names mentioned here are just a few of the families who endured the hardships and met the challenges of surviving and thriving in a place where irrigation and water supply issues were constant concerns.[3]

In the 1960s in Apple Valley, many of the homestead houses that had been built to satisfy the government requirements were still scattered throughout the valley. Most of them are gone now, but it is fortunate that historians have recorded many of the memories and documents of that important era.

The Cory family homesteaded in 1902, this view is four years later, 1906.

Water tanks, like the Holbrook family tank, stored water to provide a cool swim and to water fruit trees, circa 1913.

The Phillips homestead, 1908.

Milking the goat on a windy day at the Hitchcock Ranch homestead at Highway 18 and Navajo Road, Apple Valley, 1915.

NOTES

[1] Edward Leo Lyman, *History of Victor Valley* (Victorville, CA: Mohahve Historical Society, 2010), 149.

[2] http://www.cr.nps.gov/nr/twhp/wwwlps/lessons/67hornbeck/67setting.htm

[3] For an in-depth discussion of homesteading in the Victor Valley and the challenges faced by early settlers, see Dr. Lyman's Chapter Seven: "Hopes and Disappointments in the Era of Homesteading." 149-175.

Broader view of
the ranch, by
unknown artist.

The Hobby House
painting by
Molly Kohlschreiber.

Another Hobby House
painting by
Virginia Johnson.

Roland Boynton, Kansas Attorney General 1930-1935.

SIDE STORIES

Here are some stories and tidbits found along the way in my research:

1. AN UNLIKELY ELOPEMENT: A June 25, 1936 article in the *San Bernardino County Sun* declared that, "Manners, of Films, Weds Gwen Behr." When I saw that I gasped and said, "What? No way!" The article said that David Manners and Gwen Behr were married secretly and were now on a honeymoon trip to Canada.   But the next day a follow-up article on June 26, 1936 in the *Sun* stated that a close friend of Gwen's and her mother, Catherine Boynton, were both "positive" that no wedding had taken place.

2. A SANCTUARY FROM THE NAZIS: "French State Star, Refugees from Nazis, Meet on Desert." A July 19, 1941 *San Bernardino County Sun* article reported that Jeannine Crispin, a Parisian stage and screen actress who had fled from the Nazis in Paris, had found sanctuary at the Rancho Yucca Loma, where she was learning English. But one night she became restless and drove into Victorville to the Green Spot Inn, hangout for local cowboys, truck drivers and construction men. There she met up with some of her Parisian friends who had purchased the popular local hangout, the Green Spot, as a haven from the Nazis. That evening her husband, Georges Kessel, a screen writer, drove up from Hollywood to join the friends (and to protect his interests?).

3. DESERT RUNWAY: "Three Escape Injury as Plane Crashes." The December 17, 1951 *Los Angeles Times* reported that three men escaped injury when their plane crashed near the Yucca Loma after skimming over the top of an automobile and crashing into a tree. In Helen Berger's talk to a Victor Valley College Local History class in 1991, she mentioned that she saw the crash just as she was leaving the ranch that evening.

4. SMALL TOWN FRIENDLY DISPUTE: Several newspaper articles in 1922 exploited an ongoing feud between Catherine Boynton's cousin, William Allen White, and the Governor of Kansas, H.J. Allen. White was the owner and editor of *The Emporia* (Kansas) *Gazette*. He and the governor had been good friends.   But in July, 1922, in the middle of a railroad strike, some of the workmen distributed posters in sympathy with the strikers. When Mr. White displayed the placards in the window, he was threatened with arrest by the governor, who called the action a "form of picketing," a misdemeanor under the Industrial Court Act. The case was referred to County Attorney Roland (Billy) Boynton, Catherine Boynton's son, who issued a warrant for the arrest. The

warrant charged that Mr. White, "hindered, delayed, interfered with and suspended operation of trains on the Atchison, Topeka & Santa Fe Railroad." The case, called "Henry and Me," went on for several months until it was dismissed in December. It seemed that most of the community and the courts were tired of the whole dispute. The newspapers did not note whether or not the Governor and Mr. White remained friends. Catherine managed to still have good relations with her son and her cousin after the controversy died down.

"White Case to Supreme Court." *The Chanute Daily Tribune*, July 22, 1922.
"Placard will be Withdrawn Pending Trial." *The San Bernardino County Sun*, July 23, 1922.
"White Chesty Because Allen Got 'Yellow'." *Arkansas City Daily Traveler*, Dec. 11, 1922.

5. A HORSE NAMED "YUCCA LOMA:" The August 10 and 22, 1949 and September 10, 1949 *San Bernardino County Sun* listed a horse with the name of "Yucca Loma" in the Del Mar Handicap. This was about the time Newt Bass was establishing himself as an investor in Apple Valley. Since Newt was known to have an interest in horses and horse racing, I assumed that this was his horse. I asked Barbara Davisson, who worked for Bass for many years, if she knew about that, but she said she didn't start working for him until 1957 and hadn't heard of it. I couldn't find any reference to a horse named "Yucca Loma" after that, but he must have been a competitor, since the jockey riding him was the famous Willie Shoemaker.

6. YUCCA LOMA ROAD WAS FIRST CALLED COCAPAH STREET: The April 9, 1951 *San Bernardino County Sun* reported that the County Planning Commissioner authorized a change in name of Cocapah Street in the Apple Valley Estates, to Yucca Loma Road. Perhaps this was about the time the dirt road was paved. There is now a short stretch of Cocapah Road close to the Mojave River in Apple Valley.

David Manners with Gwen Behr and Judith Waller.

Green Spot Inn, 1940s.

The Pueblo drawing on note card.
(Donated by Joan Lopez.)

EPILOGUE - SUMMER OF 1967

Hazel Stearns, a recent member of our Mohahve Historical Society, mentioned at a meeting that she had lived at the Yucca Loma Ranch. Naturally I was skeptical, because this attractive lady was obviously too young to have lived there unless it was when she was a child. But I was curious, and we met for lunch. And I was pleasantly surprised!

Hazel grew up in Hesperia after her parents moved there in 1950. Her father was a water well driller and pipeline contractor, and her mother a real estate broker. Hazel got married and moved away; however, she returned with her husband and three children in 1967. They were looking for a house that was unique, and happened to drive by the abandoned buildings where the ranch had been. She heard that Newt Bass now owned the property, but was advised to talk to his brother, Red Bass, so she went to see him and asked if her family could live there. He told her the houses were not habitable, but she explained that her father had checked them out and said they were livable since they still had access to water and electricity. Her father had done pipeline work for Bass' company, so he approved it and rented two houses on the property to the family at $125 a month.

They moved onto the formerly Yucca Loma property at the beginning of summer. At first, the children, nine, eight, and seven, complained about the lack of air conditioning, no TV, and no friends to play with. But they soon learned to love the freedom, playing cowboys and Indians throughout the ranch, sneaking around behind the deserted cook house, Joshua trees, junipers, and sagebrush.

The family's living quarters were in a Spanish-styled adobe house. It had three very large rooms, each with a Kiva fireplace, one bath, a large walk-in closet, and a small utility room with a water heater and a sink. The other house was a pueblo-styled building that faced north on Yucca Loma. To reach it, they had to walk up a small hill behind the Spanish house.

In the Pueblo (see photo), there were four separate bedrooms, each with a full bath, two on the east side and two on the west side, with "pine vigas above to make an informal portal in the wide space in between," as Ann Rivers Sudlow described it. The family used one room for a kitchen, one as a laundry room, another for living quarters for a live-in nanny/housekeeper, and fourth for their publishing company office. Hazel described their first night in the Spanish-style house:

"We arrived late with the moving truck, and it was dark by the time we unloaded. I told the kids we were going to 'camp' in the house that night, and we'd set up the beds the next day. We cleaned an area in the middle of the large living room, put the mattresses down, and topped them with our sleeping bags. The next morning I was the first one up, and I could see for miles across the Valley through a large west-facing window. I walked to the big, arched, thick, wooden front door next to the window, and with two hands, tugged it open, ready to breathe in the fresh morning air. Instead, I jumped back and screamed as three-inch scorpions fell around my feet. They lined the entire arched area of the old door, and none of us would have slept a wink if we'd known they were there. Because we had unloaded through the back, we'd had no reason to open the front door. The view was fabulous, the history exciting, and the old adobe was loaded with charm, but age had taken its toll. Besides the venomous scorpions, tiny ants crawled out of every electrical outlet and light bulb socket in a steady stream, and worn-out water pipes frequently broke and flooded the house. But even with the creepy insects and the incessant cleanups, we were never sorry for the summer we spent at Yucca Loma Ranch."

Interior living quarters.

128

Hazel Stearns' photo of the house where they lived in 1967.

The pueblo 1940.

Hazel Stearns' children: Billy, Donny and Tana in
1967.

When Gwen Behr passed away she had left the ranch property to her
step-father, Lyman Thayer, and friends David Manners and Mildred Strong
DeMott. In April, 1956, the *San Bernardino County Sun* reported that Newt
Bass and his wife Virginia bought 520 acres in Apple Valley from the owners.
The purchase was made in three parcels of 320, 120 and 80 acres apiece. It was
not until the early 1970s that the remaining structures on the ranch were razed
for future construction.

TIMELINE--VICTOR VALLEY THE FIRST FIFTY YEARS

1900-1910:

- The town of Victor changed its name to Victorville, which became a distribution center for the many active mines of the region.
- After the first bridge at the Mojave Narrows burned, a second one was built in 1902.
- A fight for water rights threatened the Victor Valley with businesses and other places trying to divert the Mojave River.
- Cowboys from the numerous cattle ranches staged a rodeo as part of the Fourth of July celebration.
- Dances at the large town hall in Victorville drew people from Hesperia, Oro Grande, and surrounding areas.
- In 1909, Willie Boy, who had lived and worked at the North Verde Ranch, shot and killed the father of a young girl he kidnapped, leading to a 500-mile search.
- By 1910 some of the towns had voted to prohibit alcohol sales.
- The Golden State Cement Company was established in Oro Grande.
- Families came to homestead and settled on their property, and the first school in Apple Valley was established in 1910.

1911-1920:

- Catherine Boynton and Katharine Evans began the homesteading process on the land that was to become the Yucca Loma.
- By the fall of 1912 there were twelve well-drilling companies in operation, as a result of a growing number of land entries.
- The Southern Sierras Power Company had provided electric power to Victorville by 1915.
- There was a large effort to develop an irrigation system for the area.
- The inventor of the Hotpoint electric iron, Earl H. Richardson, founded Adelanto in 1915.
- The First National Bank in Victorville moved to its new building in 1918.
- The increased ownership of automobiles led to improved roads.
- By the end of 1918, 117 valley men had gone to fight in the first World War.
- Prohibition had become a national law by 1919, but most places in the Victor Valley had become dry before that.

1921-1930:
- In Clifford Walker's book, *One Eye Closed, the Other Red*, he described how the desert's "water, isolation and labor created the three ingredients for favorable moonshine operations" during the Prohibition years.
- The fight to keep Mojave River water continued.
- The Rainbow Bridge in the Mojave Narrows was completed in 1928.
- The cement industry grew to be of vital importance to local economy.
- Rodeos became popular, drawing visitors from far-away places.
- Hollywood film makers discovered the scenic desert background, and good weather provided a great venue to make movies.
- Victor Valley became a substantial fruit producing center.
- By 1929, the stock market crash marked the beginning of The Great Depression.
- As the number of visitors increased, more cottages were built, and a tennis court and swimming pool were added on Yucca Loma property.

1931-1940:
- During The Great Depression, the bank in Victorville closed its doors for a short time, but because of the small population at the time, people watched out for each other: stores allowed citizens to continue to buy food; businesses went out of their way to adjust workers' hours so that more could be employed; and those who could donated to the unemployed.
- Locals were hired as walk-ons in many of the films shot locally.
- After Prohibition was repealed in 1932, saloons were quickly opened in Victorville.
- The great flood of 1938 wiped out at least twenty-five homes in the section of Victorville between the tracks and the river. The railroad tracks in the Mojave Narrows were left hanging, and the devastation was wide-spread.
- Gwen Behr and others from the ranch became involved in community flood-relief programs and campaigns to help those affected by the flood. Even some of the guests offered their services and monetary relief.

1941-1950:

- In 1941, many valley residents became trained in how to differentiate between friendly planes and enemy planes by studying silhouettes. Unpaid volunteers were stationed at the Mojave Narrows and other strategic places with binoculars and telephones to watch for unusual activity. After the bombing of Pearl Harbor, all of the Southland was ordered to be blacked out for a short time.
- Instead of her usual guests, Gwen Behr made the Yucca Loma a place where the men and women from the Victorville Army Air Field were welcome, and where many of them stayed during the war years.
- In 1940, the Sixth Annual Victor Valley Rodeo was held at the Ihmsen Ranch, attended by over 4,000 spectators. Rodeos continued to attract visitors each year.
- By 1946, Newt Bass and Bud Westlund had begun selling Apple Valley Ranchos one-acre home sites adjacent to Highway 18.
- Katharine Evans, who was one of the original homesteaders of Rancho Yucca Loma, died in 1944.

1950-1970:

- Sadly, Rancho Yucca Loma founder Catherine Boynton passed away in 1951, and her daughter Gwen Behr succumbed to cancer in January, 1954. Her friends David Manners, stepfather Dr. Thayer, and Mildred Strong DeMott inherited the ranch.
- In 1956 Newt Bass paid $300,000 for 520 acres of the property. Some buildings were destroyed in the 1960s. By early 1970s, most of the buildings were gone, to be replaced with new homes.

> *"Modern ruins are more sorrowful than ancient ones."*
> *-Ann Rivers Sudlow*

The first bank in the Victor Valley was the First National Bank at the corner of 6th and D Streets in Victorville, opened in 1917.

The Ihmsen Ranch won first prizes in apples, pears and plums at the L.A. County Fair in 1926 and 1927.

Southwestern Portland Cement Company, 1926.

Victorville rodeo in the 1920s included the rugged steer riding event.

4—007

Form approved by the Secretary of the Interior December 16, 1911.

DEPARTMENT OF THE INTERIOR.

U. S. Land Office,
Los Angeles, Cal.

HOMESTEAD ENTRY.

U. S. LAND OFFICE _Los Angeles Ca_ . SERIAL NO. 025948

APPLICATION. RECEIPT NO. 1552361

Fees $ 10.00 Earned ½ M'M' M.

Comm. $ 6.00

Pur. Mon. $

Test. Fees $

I, _Kath Ernie Evans_ _Female_ , a resident of _Los Angeles, Los Angeles Co. Calif_ , do hereby apply

(Give full Christian name.)   (Male or female.)

(Town, County, and State.)

to enter, under Section 2289, Revised Statutes of the United States, the

S W ¼ of the N W ¼ Sec 29 & the E ½ of N E ¼ & N E ¼ of S E ¼

Section _30_ ,

Township _5 N_ , Range _3 W_ , S.B. Meridian, containing

_160 #_ acres, within the _Los Angeles_ land district;

and I do solemnly swear that I am not the proprietor of more than 160

acres of land in any State or Territory; that I _am a native_

(Applicant must state whether native born, naturalized, or has filed declaration of intention to become a citizen. If not native born, certified copy of naturalization or

born citizen of the United States, and

declaration of intention, as case may be, must be filed with this application.)

am _unmarried & over twenty one years of age_ :

(State whether the head of a family, married or unmarried, or over twenty-one years of age, and if not over twenty-one applicant must set forth the facts which

constitute him the head of a family.)

that my post-office address is _417 Andreo Blvd Los Angeles Calif_

that this application is honestly and in good faith made for the purpose of actual settlement and cultivation, and not for the benefit of any other person, persons, or corporation; that I will faithfully and honestly endeavor to comply with all the requirements of law as to settlement, residence, and cultivation necessary to acquire title to the land applied for; that I am not acting as agent of any person, corporation, or syndicate in making this entry, nor in collusion with any person, corporation, or syndicate to give them the benefit of the land entered, or any part thereof, or the timber thereon; that I do not apply to enter the same for the purpose of speculation, but in good faith to obtain a home for myself, and that I have not directly or indirectly made, and will not make, any agreement or contract, in any way or manner, with any person or persons, corporation or syndicate whatsoever, by which the title which I may acquire from the Government of the United States will inure in whole or in part to the benefit of any person except myself. I further swear that since August 30, 1890, I have not entered and acquired title to, nor am I now claiming, under an entry made under any of the nonmineral public-land laws, an amount of land which, together with the land now applied for, will exceed in the aggregate 320 acres; and that I have not heretofore made any entry under the homestead laws, or filed a soldier's or sailor's declaratory statement, except

(Here describe former homestead entry by section, township, range, land district, and number of entry; how perfected, or if not perfected state that fact.)

that I am well acquainted with the character of the land herein applied for and with each and every legal subdivision thereof, having personally examined same; that there is not to my knowledge within the limits thereof any vein or lode or quartz or other rock in place bearing gold, silver, cinnabar, lead, tin, or copper, nor any deposit of coal, placer, cement, gravel, salt spring, or deposit of salt, nor other valuable mineral deposit; that no portion of said land is claimed for mining purposes under the local customs or rules of miners, or otherwise; that no portion of said land is worked for mineral during any part of the year by any person or persons; that said land is essentially nonmineral land, and that my application therefor is not made for the purpose of fraudulently obtaining title to mineral land; that the land is not occupied and improved by any Indian.

_175 — 85_

Posted in APR 8 1915 M.M.   _Katharine Evans_

(Sign here, with full Christian name.)

NOTE.—Every person swearing falsely to the above affidavit will be punished as provided by law for such offense. (See Sec. 125, U. S. Criminal Code, over.)

The following homestead documents of Katherine Evans are from the National Archives and Records Administration, Washington, DC.

CERTIFY that the foregoing affidavit was read to or by affiant in my presence before affiant affixed signature thereto; that affiant ~~is to me personally known~~ (or has been satisfactorily identified before me

by X papers ....);
(Give full name and post-office address.)

that I verily believe affiant to be a qualified applicant and the identical person hereinbefore described; and that said affidavit was duly subscribed and sworn to before me, at my office, in _Los Angeles_ ....
(Town.)

Los Angeles Co. Calif ...., within the ....
(County and State.)

Los Angeles .... land district, this _27th_ .... day

of _February_, 19_15_. _John D. Roche_ ,

REGISTER
(Official designation of officer.)

UNITED STATES LAND OFFICE at LOS ANGELES California.

February 27, 19_15_

I HEREBY CERTIFY that the foregoing application is for surveyed land of the class which the applicant is legally entitled to enter under Section 2289, Revised Statutes of the United States, that there is no prior valid adverse right to the same, and has this day been allowed.

John D. Roche ,

Register.

UNITED STATES CRIMINAL CODE.—CHAP. 6.

SEC. 125. Whoever, having taken an oath before a competent tribunal, officer, or person, in any case in which a law of the United States authorizes an oath to be administered, that he will testify, declare, depose, or certify truly, or that any written testimony, declaration, deposition, or certificate by him subscribed, is true, shall willfully and contrary to such oath state or subscribe any material matter which he does not believe to be true, is guilty of perjury, and shall be fined not more than two thousand dollars and imprisoned not more than five years. (Act, March 4, 1909. 35 Stat., 1111.) c 6—771

Patent to contain reservation according
to proviso to the act of Aug. 30, 1890.
4—189.

Com. Hd., Act May 20, 1862.

C.H.

NHG

Department of the Interior,

United States Land Office Los Angeles, California.

Commuted Hd.

'ees $ *10 00*

omm. $ *6 00* Earned "M" H.B.

ur. Mon. $ *200 00*

e. Fees $ *2 00*

Serial No. 025943

Receipt No. 1552361

1855166

Certificate.

December 15, 1916
(Date.)

It is hereby certified that, in pursuance of law,

KATHARINE EVANS

residing at Victorville

in San Bernardino County, State of California

on this day purchased of the Register of this Office the

SW¼NW¼. Sec. 29

E½NE¼, NE¼SE¼, Section 30

Township 5 N., Range 3 W., S.B. Meridian,

California, containing 160 Acres,

at the rate of One Dollar and Twenty-five Cents

per acre, amounting to Two Hundred Dollars

and no Cents, for which the said

Katharine Evans

has made payment in full as required by law.

Now, therefore, be it known that, on presentation of this

Certificate to the COMMISSIONER OF THE GENERAL LAND OFFICE, the

said

Katharine Evans

shall be entitled to receive a Patent for the land above described,
if all then appear regular.

John D. Roche, Register.

NOTE.—A duplicate of this Certificate is issued to the claimant as notice of the acceptance of the proof and payment, and of the allowance of the entry by the Register and Receiver.
The original is forwarded to the General Land Office, with the entry papers, for approval by the Commissioner of the General Land Office and issuance of patent.
The duplicate copy forwarded to the claimant should be held until notice of issuance of patent is received.
In all correspondence concerning the entry in connection with which this Certificate issued, refer to the NAME OF THE LAND OFFICE and the SERIAL NUMBER noted hereon.

PAT NO 582754
MAY 4 1917

X APPROVED *Apr. 4/17*

6—1719

By *R. J. Deit*, Division C

Posted in 175/85 Feb. 6, 1917. P.T. "D"

138

For use in
HOMESTEAD and
DESERT LAND
Entries.

4—348

NOTICE OF INTENTION TO MAKE PROOF.

DEPARTMENT OF THE INTERIOR,

U. S. LAND OFFICE at _____

_____, 191

I, __Katharine Evans_____, of

__Victorville, California_____, who, on ___February 27___, 191 5, made

__HOMESTEAD__ Entry _____, No. __025943___, for
          (Kind of application or entry.)

{ SW 1/4 of NW 1/4 Section 29 and
  _____, Section_____,
  East half of NE 1/4 and NE 1/4 of SE 1/4 Section 30

Township __5 N____, Range __3 W____, ___San Bernardino_____Meridian,

hereby give notice of my intention to make ____Commutation____
                    (If homestead, insert "five-year," "three-year," or "commutation," as case may be.)

Proof, to establish my claim to the land above described, before

__Register and Receiver_____, at
          (Name of officer.)

__Los Angeles California_____, on the ___15___ day of

__Dec_____, 191 6, by two of the following witnesses:

__Dr. Harris Garcelon_____, of ___Victorville , California___

__William Addison Foster_____, of ___Victorville , California___

__Alfred Merle Byron_____, of ___Victorville , California___

__Mrs. William Addison Foster___, of ___Victorville , California.___

Katharine Evans,
(Signature of claimant.)

_____, 191

Notice of the above intention to make proof will be published in the

News Herald   *Victorville, Cal*
(Name of newspaper.)   (Place of publication.)

for a period of_____consecutive_____, which I hereby designate

as the newspaper published nearest the land above described.

John D. Roche,
Register.

6—2657

139

4—196

Department of the Interior

United States Land Office ___ Los Angeles, Cal. _____

Fees $ _10._____
Comm (Orig)$ _6._____
Excess $ _____
Comm (Fin.) $ _6._____
Pur Mon $ _____
Test Fees $ _7._____
Interest $ _____
_EM_

Serial No. _____ 032114
Receipt No. _____ 2279936
2531621 5/9/22

Final Certificate.

Homestead.

Sec. 7, Act 2-19-09

Patent to contain reservation according
to proviso to the Act of Aug. 30, 1890.

_____ May 9 _____, 19 22
(Date.)

It is hereby certified that, pursuant to the provisions of Section 2291, Revised Statutes of the United States,
Katharine Evans,

_____ Victorville, Cal.,_____

has made payment in full for _____

N½SW¼; SE¼NW¼; SW¼NE¼ _____ Section _____ 29

Township _____ 5 N. ___, Range _ 3 W. ___, _____ S. B. Meridian

California _____, containing _____ 160 _____ acres.

Now, therefore, be it known that, on presentation of this
Certificate to the COMMISSIONER OF THE GENERAL LAND OFFICE, the
said _____ Katharine Evans

shall be entitled to receive a Patent for the land above described
if all then be found regular.

_____, Register.

NO RESERVATION 1-12-192

PAT NO 873562 July 24 1922

NOTE.—A duplicate of this Certificate is issued to the claimant as notice of the acceptance of the proof and payment, and of the allowance of the entry by the Register and
Receiver.
    The original is forwarded to the General Land Office, with the entry papers, for
approval by the Commissioner of the General Land Office and issuance of patent.
    The duplicate copy forwarded to the claimant should be held until notice of issuance
of patent is received.
    In all correspondence concerning the entry in connection with which this Certificate is
issued, refer to the NAME OF THE LAND OFFICE and the SERIAL NUMBER noted hereon.

Posted _June 28 1922_ In Vol _175_, P. _85_, by _____, Div. "O."

APPROVED _July 15 1922_

4—196 By _____ L. French _____, Division _6_

140

SOURCES - Most are on file at the Victor Valley College Library

Notes from Evelyn O'Brien's Research:

Includes notes on phone conversations with Betty Lasky and Dorothy Denny, both of whom spent time on the Yucca Loma when they were young. Evelyn found many newspaper articles relating to the ranch; photos were obtained from various people she contacted. Her papers were donated to the Victor Valley College Library collection.

Author's Interviews with Local "Old-Timers who remember the Rancho Yucca Loma:"

Patricia Bergen - Ella Cardenas - Barbara Davisson - Shirley Davisson - Felix Diaz - Dick Garrison - Diane and Tom Irwin - Robert Powell - Hazel Stearns - Ellsworth Sylvester.

Unpublished Manuscripts:

Barry, John. *Early Days in Apple Valley*, n.d.
Barry, John. *Yucca Loma*, n.d.
Barry, Nini. *Catherine Boynton*, one-page biography, n.d.
DeBlasis, Jean. *A Brief History of the [Kemper Campbell] Ranch*, n.d.
Mendel interview. Two-page history of *Mendel Ranch*, 1985 or 1986.
Sudlow, Ann Rivers. *Rancho Yucca Loma*, July 2001.

Transcriptions of Oral Interviews in the Victor Valley College Library:

DeMott, Mildred. *Interview #4*, 12/4/70.
Jess, Stoddard Interview. *#214, 6/21/88; #215, 6/30/88.*
Kirkpatrick, Paul. *Interview #59*, 4/9/74.
Stockdale, Allison. *Interview #124*, 5/29/98.
White, Hazel. *Interview #24*, May 1971.

E-mail Correspondence: Patricia Bergen - Gary Ledford - Jill Huettner & Joy Kirkpatrick (daughters of Paul & Eleanor Kirkpatrick).

Obituaries:

Barry, Elizabeth "Betsy:" "Daily Press Loses Founding Family Member," *Daily Press*, February 17, 2014.
Barry, John: "John Barry, Founder of Daily Press, Dies at 89," *Daily Press*, December 1, 1995.
Barry, Nini: "Press' Co-Founder Nini Barry Passes," *Victor Press*, August 25,1955.
Boynton, Catherine: *Victor Press*, July 1, 1949.
"Marie Chapule Dead at 104," Daily Press, July 14, 1966.
DeMott, Mildred: April 9, 1894-February 4, 1973 (*Ancestry.com*)
Denny, Dorothy: *Daily Press*, January 18, 2007.
Evans, Katharine: *Victor Valley News Herald*, June, 1944.
Manners, David: *Los Angeles Times,* December 26, 1998.
Thayer, Dr. Lyman: *Los Angeles Times*, October, 1960.

Brochures:

C Bar Ranch - Mac Dude Ranch - Sky-Hi Ranch - Victor Valley, the All Year Desert Resort , 1940.
    Victor Valley Chamber of Commerce, Victorville, 1949.

<u>Maps</u>: The hand-drawn insurance map of Yucca Loma by Gwendolyn Behr was donated by Maggie Cramer.   Rhonda Almager and Jean Williams at the Victor Valley Museum found the 1956 topographic map of Yucca Loma. Larry Reese arranged the maps to show them side by side for comparison. A 1968 AAA map of Victor Valley was used to indicate the areas covered.

<u>Reference Books:</u>

American National Biography. New York: Oxford University Press. "Maude Adams," Vol. 1; "Ernest Thompson Seton," Vol. 19; "William Allen White," Vol. 23.

Contemporary Authors. Detroit: Gale Research, Inc. "Edwin Corle," Vol. 178; "William Roderick James," Vol. 19; "Bierne Lay, Jr.," Vol. 107; "Jess Oppenheimer," Vol. 127; "Mary Roberts Rinehart," Vol. 166.

Contemporary Black Biography. Farmington Mills, MI: Gale Group, 2002. "Eddie 'Rochester' Anderson," Vol. 30.

Current Biography. New York: The H.W. Wilson Company. "Jack Benny," 1963; "Gower & Marge Champion," 1953; "Hedda Hopper," 1942; "Irwin Shaw," 1943.

Dictionary of American Biography. New York: Charles Scribner's Sons. "George Vernon Denny, Jr.," Supp.4; "Tony Sarg," Supp. 3; "William Allen White," Vol. 9.

The Dictionary of Art. Grove, 1996. "Alfredo Ramos Martinez."

The Encyclopedia of Hollywood. New York: Facts on File, 1990. "Gregory Peck;" "Loretta Young;" "Fred Zinnemann."

The Film Encyclopedia. New York: Thomas Crowell, 1969. "Sy Bartlett;" "Priscilla Lane;" "Arthur Lubin;" "Cesar Romero."

Gale Encyclopedia of Biography. Detroit: Gale Research. "Jesse Lasky."

The Great Stage Directors. New York: Facts on File, 1994. "George Abbott; "Rouben Mamoulian."

International Dictionary of Films & Filmmakers 2: Directors, 3rd edition. Detroit: St. James Press, 1997. "Dorothy Arzner."

International Dictionary of Films & Filmmakers 3: Actors & Actresses. "Beulah Bondi;" "Clark Gable;" "Bill Holden."

International Dictionary of Films & Filmmakers 4: Writers & Production Artists. "Daniel Taradash."

Magill's Survey of Cinema. First Series, Vol. 2. Englewood Cliffs, N.J.: Salem Press, 1980. "Lewis Meltzer--Golden Boy."

The New Grove Dictionary of Music & Magicians, 2nd edition, Vol. 3. London: Macmillan Publishers, 2001. "Carrie Jacobs-Bond."

New York Times Directory of the Film. New York: Arno Press, 1971. "David Manners."

<u>Books:</u>

Corle, Edwin. *Desert Country*. New York: Duell, Sloan & Pearce, 1941.

Lyman, Edward Leo. *History of Victor Valley*. Victorville, CA: Mohahve Historical Society, 2010.

Mohahve I. Victorville: Victor Valley College, 1963.

McCullough, David. *Mornings on Horseback*. New York: Simon & Schuster, 1981.

Rinehart, Mary Roberts. *Through Glacier Park*. Boston: Houghton Mifflin Co., 1916.

Small, George Raphael. *Ramos Martinez: His Life and Art*. Westlake Village, CA: F & J Publishing Corp., 1975.

Thompson, Richard D. *Elmore and Harriet Corwin and the Corwin Ranch*. Apple Valley: Desert Knolls Press, 2002.

Thompson. *Murray's Ranch: Apple Valley's African-American Dude Ranch*. Apple Valley: Desert Knolls Press, 2002.

Walker, Cliff. One *Eye Closed, the Other Red: The California Bootlegging Years*. Back Door Publishing, 1999.

Photographs:

The Mohahve Historical Society Collection; Evelyn O'Brien; Ann Rivers Sudlow; the Kirkpatrick sisters and previous photos donated by Eleanor Kirkpatrick; Hazel Stearns; Patricia Bergen; *Kingdom of the Sun* publication; Series of three articles in the *Daily Press* in October, 1968, and others. Many of the photos of poor quality were skillfully transformed by Larry Reese.

Periodical Articles:

Borne, Lawrence R. "Dude Ranching and the Development of the West," *Journal of the West*,
    July 1978, 83-84.
Gilbert, Bill. "Black Wolf," *Smithsonian*, July 1997, 110+.
Kingdom of the Sun. 1912 and 1913.
Lesure, Thomas. "Dude Ranching…the Western Vacation Few Westerners Ever Take,"
    Desert Magazine, December, 1960, 26-28.

Internet Sources:

Ancestry.com: for obituaries and census records.
"Herman Behr, Jr. married Gwendolyn Boynton, December 1, 1917 at Greenwich, Connecticut."
    New York Social Register, May 1920, 50.
Boynton, Catherine. *Biographical Cyclopedia of American Women*, Vol. II 1924.
Norris, John. *David Manners Biography*, accessed 2/9/2013.
"Romance, Rest & Recreation."
    http://www.lib.virginia.edu/etd/theses/ArtsSci/English/1998/Zimmerman.
Manners, David: http://membersaol.com/rickmckay/DavidMan.html, 7/12/2006.
    http://www.davidmanners.com/biography.html, 1/17/2013.

Newspaper Articles:

"Air Cadets Show Skill Making Beds." *Los Angeles Times*, November 12, 1942.
Couey, William. "Sage Hens Ranch Meets Quick End." *Daily Press*, January 16, 1987.
Couey. "Sage Hens Ranch: The Place is Still There, but the Good Times Are Gone." *Daily Press*,
    February 22, 1985.
Jacobs, Bob. "Planes May Hum Again Over Old Guest Ranch." *Daily Press*, June 15, 1969.
Landis, Mark. "Dude, Where's My Ranch?" *San Bernardino Sun*, June 17, 2008.
Lombardo, Lynnea. "Wife of Daily Press Founder Turns 100." *Daily Press*, July 16, 2012.
"Lone Wolf Colony: A Place to Get Well." *Daily Press*, May 22, 1968.
"Pioneer Woman." *Daily Press*, May 3, 1985.
[Poates, Ursula]. *San Bernardino County Sun*, May 16, 1911.
"Placard Will be Withdrawn Pending Trial." *The San Bernardino County Sun*, July 23, 1922.
Ryan, Harriet. "A Big Donor Despite Dementia." *Los Angeles Times*, April 9, 2012.
"White Case to Supreme Court." *The Chanute Daily Tribune*, July 22, 1922.
"White Chesty Because Allen Got 'Yellow'." *Arkansas City Daily Traveler*, December 11, 1922.
"Woodcraft Program." *San Bernardino County Sun*, March 29, 1922.

Video recording:

Helen Berger spoke to a Victor Valley Local History Class on March 17, 1994 on her memories of the Yucca Loma Ranch. VHS recording is in VVC Library.

VICTOR VALLEY COLLEGE LOCAL HISTORY COLLECTION

Most of the materials accessed for this book are in the Victor Valley College Local History Room files. In addition to those cited, here are some of the other references available for additional research on Victor Valley history. This is just a sampling:

Banks, L.A. "Buzz." *Policing the Old Mojave Desert*. Victorville: Buzz Banks, 1994.

Bowen, Gertie & Warren D. *Bowen Escapades*. Apple Valley, CA, 1950.

DeBlasis, Celeste. *Graveyard Peaches: A California Memoir*. New York: St. Martin's Press, 1991.

Diaz, Felix. *Footprints on the Mojave: A View From the Barrio*. Victorville: Diaz, 2007.

Gobar, Julian Smith. *Raising the Dust* [Lucerne Valley history]. St. George, Utah, 1969.

Hampton, Mary. *Our Apple Valley--A Chatty Guide*. Apple Valley: Apple Valley News, 1967.

LaFuze, Pauliena. *Saga of the San Bernardinos*. San Bernardino County Museum Association, 1971.

Lyman, Edward Leo. *History of Victor Valley*. Victorville: Mohahve Historical Society, 2010.

Mohahve I (parts 1and 2). Victorville: Victor Valley College, 1963.

Mohahve II. Victorville: Mohahve Historical Society, 1965.

Mohahve III. Victorville: Mohahve Historical Society, 1966.

Mohahve IV. Victorville: Mohahve Historical Society, 1984.

Mohahve V. Victorville: Mohahve Historical Society, 1991.

Mohahve VI. Victorville: Mohahve Historical Society, 2011.

O'Rourke, Kate. *The History of Apple Valley: From Early Man to 2004*. Apple Valley: Lewis Center for Educational Research, 2004.

Thompson, Richard D. *Murray's Ranch: Apple Valley's African-American Dude Ranch*. Desert Knolls Press, 2002.

Thompson, Richard D. *Pioneer of the Mojave: The Life and Times of Aaron G. Lane*. Apple Valley: Desert Knolls Press, 2002.

Thompson, Richard D. *The Story of Sagebrush Annie and the Sagebrush Route*. Apple Valley: Desert Knolls Press, 2011.

Walker, Clifford. *Back Door to California: The Story of the Mojave River Trail*. Barstow, CA: Mojave River Valley Museum Association, 1986.

The collection consists of historical maps, old newspapers on microfilm, oral history tapes and transcripts, numerous subject files, photographs, manuscripts, and rare books on desert history. Subject files cover such topics, as railroads, mining, schools, ranches, businesses, development, plants, animals, geology, water issues, land use, and history of people and towns. Oral histories include interviews from the early 1970s of old-timers who had lived in the Victor Valley as far back as the early 1900s.

Also: Some of Richard Thompson's writings may be found at his website: mojavehistory.com.

RANCHO YUCCA LOMA INDEX

The Manners house at Rincon and Waco has been named
"Historical Point of Interest" by the Town of Apple Valley.

Made in the USA
San Bernardino, CA
17 September 2017